DON
-2020

5

DELMARVA'S PATTY CANNON

DELMARVA'S PATTY CANNON

The Devil on the Nanticoke

MICHAEL MORGAN

THE
History
PRESS

Published by The History Press
Charleston, SC 29403
www.historypress.net

First published 2015

ISBN 978.1.62619.812.8

Library of Congress Control Number: 2015935125

Notice: The information in this book is true and complete to the best of our knowledge. It is offered without guarantee on the part of the author or The History Press. The author and The History Press disclaim all liability in connection with the use of this book.

Contents

Contents

Preface

When my editor, Hannah Cassilly, at The History Press first suggested Patty Cannon as a topic, I was hesitant. As any longtime resident of Maryland and Delaware knows, the crimes of Patty Cannon are legendary, and I was concerned that her criminal actions, like legends of pirates' buried treasure, had increased as the tales were passed down over the generations. In addition, knowing that criminals were not apt to publicize their actions, I believed that it would be difficult to find contemporary documentation of her activities. I was wrong on both counts. Patty's heinous crimes equal—if not surpass—the legends, and her robberies, kidnappings and murders were reported in newspapers, books, diaries and court documents as they happened. This book is a result of the distillation of the early nineteenth-century records that reveal the reality of the crimes of Patty Cannon before the legend had a chance to grow.

The crimes of Patty Cannon are documented in numerous libraries, archives and museums, and it would not have been possible to write this book without the assistance of the dedicated people who staff these institutions, including the Laurel Public Library and the Talbot County Free Library in Easton. In particular, I would like to thank Jim Blackwell of the Seaford Historical Society for answering my many questions and allowing me to photograph the Patty Cannon display in the society's museum. I also would like to thank the staff of the Delaware Public Archives for their help in locating documents pertinent to Patty's criminal career. Randy L. Goss, coordinator of accessing and processing/photo archivist/preservation

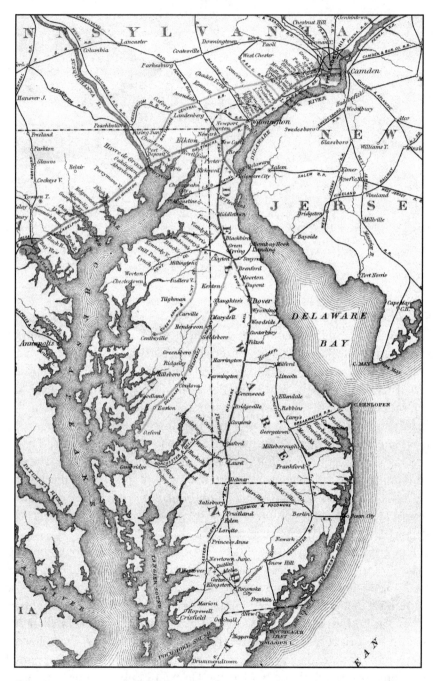

The Delmarva Peninsula where Patty Cannon and her cohort of cutthroats robbed, kidnapped and murdered in the early nineteenth century. *Courtesy of the Delaware Public Archives.*

officer at the archives, was instrumental in providing many of the images in this book. I would also like to thank my son, Tom, and his wife, Karla, for their support and technical assistance. Finally, I would like to thank my wife, Madelyn, for her constant editorial advice and support. She read every word in this book numerous times and spent countless hours correcting my spelling, punctuation and grammar. Without her help and support, this book would not have been possible.

Chapter 1
A Criminal's World

DRESSED IN MEN'S ATTIRE

Tall, dark and flirty, Patty Cannon captivated her guests, a slave trader named Ridgell and his traveling companion, as she poured another hot apple toddy. The two had stopped at Cannon's house, and Patty, a woman with long dark hair, invited Ridgell to discuss business, be served strong drinks and talk about other things. Ridgell had money to buy slaves, and Patty said that she had a slave to sell—but enough of that. The slave was not here at the moment, so she invited her guests to have another drink. Before long, the sun was setting, and Ridgell allowed that he must be going. Perhaps they could meet in Laurel to complete the transaction. With that, the slave trader and his companion boarded their carriage and started down the road to Laurel.

The moment the carriage left the Cannon house, Patty; her son-in-law, Harry Brereton (a notorious kidnapper from Lewes); and two brothers with checkered pasts, John and Jesse Griffith, knew what they needed to do. Patty changed her dress to men's clothing. The men and Patty donned dark greatcoats and tall hats and armed themselves with muskets and other weapons. Horses were brought from the stables, and the four riders headed for Laurel, an island in a dark sea of forest.

In the second decade of the nineteenth century, Laurel, the principal town in western Sussex County, was home to three hundred souls, several taverns,

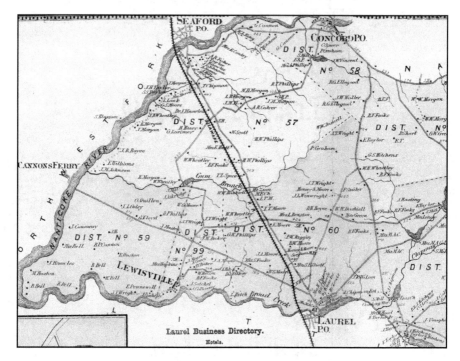

This mid-nineteenth-century map shows the Nanticoke River (running diagonally across the left side of the map), Cannon's Ferry (left center) and Laurel (bottom center). Johnson's Crossroads and Patty Cannon's house were in the blank area on the left of the map. *Courtesy of the Delaware Public Archives.*

a few mills and a couple shipyards. Situated on Broad Creek (an eastern branch of the Nanticoke River), Laurel was tucked away in the interior of the Delmarva Peninsula, isolated from much of the outside world, including the War of 1812 that was raging between the United States and Great Britain. Ridgell and his companion could expect to find reasonable accommodations in Laurel, if they reached the town.

As the carriage bumped along the gloomy trail, the Nanticoke River, broad and deep, loomed several miles ahead. The four shadowy thugs on horseback knew that the carriage would cross the river at Cannon's Ferry and that it would take time for the ferryman to be called, the carriage loaded on the scowl and the ferry to be muscled across the waterway. If the four riders were quick, they could cross the river at Hooper's Landing (Seaford), at the head of navigation, and scamper through the woods to set their ambush. Ridgell had ready cash, and the four hoodlums of the forest meant to get it.

A modern view of the Nanticoke River and Cannon's Ferry (now known as Woodland Ferry) looking north toward Seaford. Johnson's Crossroads and Patty Cannon's House were several miles to the left of the picture. *Courtesy of the Delaware Public Archives.*

A sturdy woman, Patty was said to be fond of music and dancing and as strong as most men, but she was all feminine charm and wit a short time earlier when Ridgell and his companion were in her home. Situated on the border between Delaware and Maryland, northwest of Seaford, Patty's house often hosted travelers in that sparsely settled part of Delmarva. Patty had no qualms about entertaining the two slave traders, some of the least-esteemed people in the early nineteenth century. Although slavery was legal in Delaware, some looked with contempt on those who bought and sold humans for a living. Knowing that the traders carried cash to expedite their purchases, Patty had gladly made flirty small talk over glasses of wine and apple toddies. After the last glass was emptied, the traders bid their adieu, mounted their carriage and started down the road toward Laurel, taking the most direct route that bypassed Seaford and would cross the Nanticoke at Cannon's Ferry.

When the carriage disappeared from sight, Patty summoned her three cohorts, planned the ambush and galloped off to intercept the slave traders and their cash. Having crossed the river at Seaford, the four assailants headed south until they reached the road from Cannon's Ferry to Laurel. Confident that they had arrived ahead of the slave traders, Patty's gang rode to the crest of a small hill, where they cut brush from the woods and dragged it into the road. Holding their weapons upright with the butts on the ground, they quickly poured powder and shot into the muzzles and rammed the charges home. Nimbly, they cradled the muskets in their arms and filled the pans with the charging powder. Weapons loaded, the four hid and waited.

Flintlock muskets were not entirely reliable. The firing mechanism depended on a flint striking steel and creating a shower of sparks that would land in a pan of powder, ignite and burn through a touch hole to the main powder at the breach of the weapon. If all went right, that powder would ignite, and the resulting explosion would send the bullet toward its target. A strong breeze, wet powder and other conditions could cause the weapon to misfire. If all four weapons of the Cannon gang were fired at once, the ambush stood a good chance of success.

The assailants were in position when the slave traders' carriage came clip-clopping down the road. At the hilltop obstruction, the horses slowed. Patty and the others opened fire. The puff of powder in the pan was followed by the ripping crack of musket fire. The lead balls slammed into the carriage. Ridgell, severely wounded by a ball that passed through his torso, staggered out of the carriage with a pistol in his hand. Firing wildly in the dark at the concealed assassins, the slave trader failed to hit any of the Cannon

The ambush on the slave trader Ridgell by Patty and three members of her gang. Published a dozen years after her death, this incident would have grave repercussions for the Cannon-Johnson kidnappers. From the *Narrative and Confessions of Patty Cannon.*

gang. Blood gushing from his wound, Ridgell re-boarded his carriage, and the terrified horses bolted through the brush that was blocking the road. Denied an easy prey, the four highwaymen failed to pursue the carriage as it careened down the road. A short time later, Ridgell and his friend arrived at Laurel. About an hour after reaching town, Ridgell died of his wounds. His companion took small comfort that he was one of the few who had survived an attack by Patty Cannon.

A Convenient River on the East Called Kuskarawaok

Patty Cannon plied her mischief in the dense forests and low grasslands near the banks of the Nanticoke River in a criminal career that stretched across the first three decades of the nineteenth century. When most of Delmarva's rivers emptied into the Chesapeake, they were quiet waterways with low marshy banks nearly indistinguishable from the bay's broad expanse. From the bay, these rivers wound their way northeasterly across Maryland until they narrowed to small streams before they crossed into Delaware. The Nanticoke, however, was wide and deep as it flowed into the bay, and unlike the rest, the Nanticoke remained navigable along its snake-like route well into Delaware.

In 1608, Captain John Smith and fourteen other Jamestown colonists boarded a shallop (a two-masted, shallow-draft open boat, ideal for exploring creeks and rivers) and sailed across the Chesapeake Bay. On the east side of the bay, he headed north until he was pounded by an early summer thunderstorm, during which his mast and sail blew overboard. Smith repaired his sail with shirts and entered the mouth of the Nanticoke, which he described as "a pretty convenient river on the east called Kuskarawaok." Smith's small boat navigated about twenty miles of the river's wide curls before he encountered occasional firm land along the waterway's banks. Passing the future site of Vienna, Maryland, Smith saw firm land covered with forests of pine, gum and other trees and inhabited by Native Americans, who welcomed the Europeans with a volley of arrows. Smith anchored his small boat in the middle of the Nanticoke, out of range of the Indian missiles. The next day, the Englishmen made a brief excursion ashore, fired their muskets at the Native Americans and then retreated back to the Chesapeake.

After Smith returned to England, he published an account of his American adventures. Included in Smith's *The Generall Historie of Virginia, New England*

The Nanticoke River at Vienna, Maryland, an important colonial port of entry. Sloops carrying many of Patty Cannon's victims passed this way on their way to the South. *Photo by Michael Morgan.*

and the Summer Isles was a map of the places that he visited. Smith's map was the first detailed representation of the Delmarva Peninsula, and the serpentine course of the Nanticoke, which Smith called the Kuskarawaok, is clearly visible as it makes its way from the Chesapeake Bay into southern Delaware. It is not clear how far up the river Smith traveled; it is believed that he traveled as far as Broad Creek, but he may not have entered that tributary of the Nanticoke and probably did not reach the future site of Laurel. Staying in the security of his shallop, Smith also missed the Great Cypress Swamp, east of Laurel.

Two centuries ago, the Great Cypress Swamp, considered one of the natural wonders of early America, cast a dark shadow across central Delmarva. The swamp was a high and level basin, the highest ground between the Atlantic Ocean and Chesapeake Bay. The center of the fifty-thousand-acre basin was spongy, wet ground that extended six miles from east to west and nearly twelve miles from north to south. The marshy tract was so thick with cypress trees that they blotted out the sun on a cloudless day and provided a home for wolves, bears and other dangerous creatures. A nineteenth-century visitor to the swamp remarked, "As we plunged deeper into the swamp the trees increased in size. Here and there a black pool of water lay gleaming sullenly, hiding, as it were, among a thick growth of rank ferns and venomous-looking flowers. Vine-covered cypresses rose high aloft, the inevitable steamers of gray moss hanging motionlessly pendent." As for the people who lived in the swamp, they were as isolated as the wild beasts, birds and reptiles. "Here one finds the usual characteristics of pioneer swamp life—the bilious look and muddy complexion indicative of miasmatic atmosphere and hard work."

When John Smith sailed up the Nanticoke, he had no intention of leaving the river and sailing inland toward the coast. Had he done so, he would have discovered that the swamp blocked easy travel eastward from the Nanticoke to Delaware Bay, and it heightened the isolation of the forests along the river. Smith was content to remain in the safety of his shallop, perhaps as far as the head of navigation, the future site of Seaford. If he traveled that far, Smith passed the quiet stretch of the Nanticoke where Cannon's Ferry would be established.

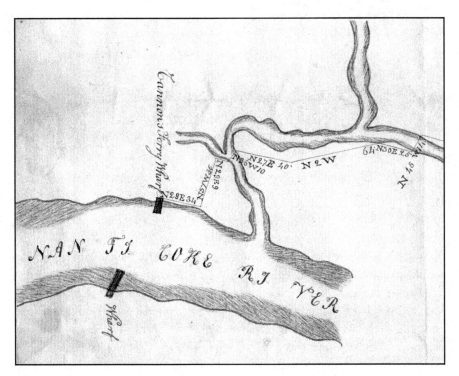

The ferry operated by James Cannon and his descendants as depicted in an early nineteenth-century map. *Courtesy of the Delaware Public Archives.*

Simplified Cannon Family Tree

(Does not include all siblings and marriages)

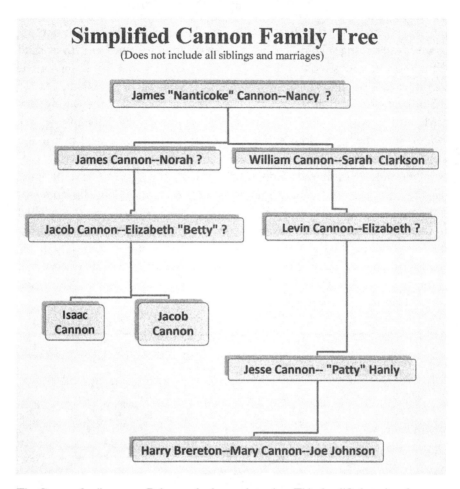

The Cannon family tree on Delmarva had many branches. This simplified version shows the relationship with the founders of the ferry and significant people mentioned in the text. *Illustration by Michael Morgan.*

In the seventeenth and eighteenth centuries, other colonists would retrace Smith's route to settle along the banks of the Nanticoke and its tributaries. The lower reaches of the Nanticoke were claimed by Maryland, and the settlers from Lord Baltimore's colony had little regard for where Maryland ended and Delaware began. Using the river as a grand highway into the wilderness, the settlers brought tobacco seeds and slaves. The colonists cleared small plots amid the forest, planted tobacco and, with the help of their slaves, pruned, weeded and nurtured the crop until the broad leaves were harvested. After curing in small, flimsy barns, the tobacco was packed into hogsheads, turned on their sides and rolled along newly cut trails to the river, to be shipped to distant ports. Gradually, the settlers of central Delmarva abandoned tobacco for other crops, but they retained their small farms and their slaves.

Among the early colonists who settled along the Nanticoke were the progenitors of the Cannon clan, whose family tree found fertile ground on Delmarva and grew into many gnarled branches that included some of the area's finest citizens and a few of the most notorious scoundrels. At several places along the Nanticoke, makeshift water crossings were established over the river, and by the middle of the eighteenth century, James Cannon operated a ferry across the river on the road from Laurel to Federalsburg, Maryland, about five miles from the Delaware border. In the late eighteenth century, Patty married a great-grandson of James Cannon, and the couple would settle in the forest west of the Nanticoke. Patty's genealogical roots were as dark as the Nanticoke forests. Some believe that she was from Canada. Others have suggested that she was from Buffalo, New York, but still others believe she was born on Delmarva. Whatever her origins, when Patty married Jesse, they moved to somewhere on the Maryland-Delaware border, a boundary that had defied demarcation throughout the colonial period.

"We Will Shoot You"

When the English colonized North America, their knowledge of the geography of the continent was uninformed, imprecise and, in some cases, utterly inaccurate. The border between Maryland, held by the Calvert family, and the lands held by the Penn family, who owned Pennsylvania and Delaware, created a legal no-man's land in the center of the Delmarva Peninsula. Patty Cannon, her cohorts and others used the imprecise boundary between the two states, Maryland and Delaware, to avoid responsibility for their actions.

In an effort to rectify the border dispute, a team of surveyors from both colonies gathered in December 1750 to begin marking the boundary. Beginning at Fenwick Island, the surveyors worked westward and ran a line across the Delmarva Peninsula to a point several miles south of Cannon's Ferry. Stones incised with the coats of arms of the Penn and Calvert families were set up at intervals to delineate the border. After the trans-peninsula line had been established, the surveying team intended to lay out the western border of Delaware, but when Lord Baltimore died in 1751, all survey work on the border stopped. A few years later, several colonists claimed to be living in Sussex County, but officials in Worcester County, Maryland, were convinced that the settlers were living on Maryland territory.

In 1759, sub-sheriff William Outten and a small posse were dispatched to the home of James Willey to arrest the colonist for failure to pay Maryland taxes. When Outten, armed with a cutlass, entered Willey's house, Willey retreated to the building's loft and refused to surrender. Some of Willey's neighbors arrived, and one declared, "Where is the damned eternal sheriff? I'll cleave him to the earth."

Just then, Outten stepped outside, and in the altercation that followed, the sheriff was shot and killed. Willey and his cohorts retreated to Lewes, beyond the Great Cypress Swamp, where they would claim that they were peacefully living in southern Delaware when they were confronted by the Maryland posse. The Lewes court concluded that the incident had happened in Maryland, and Willey was turned over to the Worcester County officials with the note, "A very unhappy and much to be lamented transaction hath lately fallen out with respect to the boundary or dividing line between this county of Sussex on Delaware and Worcester County in the province of Maryland of which your Honor will be more fully informed on perusal of the copies of the several depositions herewith sent you."

Five years after Outten's murder, Charles Mason and Jeremiah Dixon were hired to finish the work that the earlier surveyor team had begun. Mason and Dixon began at the center of the trans-peninsula line and surveyed the north–south line between Maryland and Delaware. They then established the east–west line between Maryland and Pennsylvania. The latter boundary would become famous as the Mason-Dixon Line that marked, somewhat inaccurately, the division between the free and slave states.

Setting up stone markers in the forests of Delmarva, however, did not end the border disputes. In 1774, James Mitchell Jr., fervently loyal to Delaware, was furious that settlers from Maryland were claiming parts of southern Delaware. Mitchell formed a posse, approached the cabin of Stephen Bissel and called out to Bissell, "Come outside without arms or by God, we will shoot you." After Mitchell had forced Bissell from the cabin, Mitchell had Bissell's modest possessions taken from the building and piled into the yard. Mitchell told the interlopers that if he or anyone else from Maryland ever returned to this place, they would suffer dearly. To reinforce this threat, Mitchell and his band proceeded to tear down the cabin.

This small pavilion marks the center of the transpeninsular line. Mason and Dixon began at this point and surveyed the east–west boundary between Maryland and Delaware. In the photo, Maryland is to the left, and Delaware is to the right. *Photo by Michael Morgan.*

In the pavilion at the center of the trans-peninsular line are several stone markers. The coats of arms of the Penn family, who owned Delaware at the time, and the Calvert family, the proprietors of Maryland, are incised in the markers. *Photo by Michael Morgan.*

Mitchell's rough treatment of squatters who encroached on Delaware land led Marylanders to organize a posse and retaliate. Mitchell, unperturbed, declared that he would make a stand at General John Dagworthy's estate where the general had two small cannons that he would use to "blow them to hell." Mitchell's determination to defend Delaware did not last long. The start of the American Revolution gave the colonists bigger fish to fry, but when the war was over, Jesse and Patty Cannon were free to exploit the cloudy border and the dark forests in order to inflict their misdeeds on the people living near the Nanticoke River.

THOMPSON'S BEGINNING

Patty and Jesse Cannon's neighbors were a polyglot population. A few owned substantial plantations where they lived in picturesque mansions pleasantly situated near gently flowing streams. Others lived in hardscrabble shacks built with rough-hewed timbers and dirt floors as they eked out a subsistence on small plots hemmed in by the forests. Some settlers on Delmarva had been to Oxford and other institutions of higher learning. Others were uneducated and illiterate. Most who settled on Delmarva were of European stock, but peppered among the whites were sons of Africa, slave, indentured and free.

John Johnson's father, Anthony, had been captured in Africa, thrust into chains and eventually carried to Jamestown, Virginia, at the time the only English colony in America. At Jamestown, Johnson and over twenty other Africans were sold to the English in exchange for food. Technically, the Africans were not slaves. Although they were involuntarily bound to their masters, their service was to be for a set period of time, as specified in a contract or "indenture" that required them to work to cover the cost of their purchase, plus their food and boarding. Although the white masters often ignored the terms of these contracts, Anthony Johnson eventually became a free man, and by 1651, he owned 250 acres of land with five servants of his own. In addition, Anthony and his wife, Mary, had two sons and two daughters.

Anthony Johnson and his family moved to Northampton County on Virginia's Eastern Shore, and in 1665, they moved to Somerset County, Maryland, where they settled on Wicomico Creek, south of the Nanticoke River. Anthony passed away sometime before 1670, and one of his sons, John, left Maryland and moved to Delaware, where he acquired a substantial tract of four hundred acres on Rehoboth Bay.

For the next three decades, John Johnson appeared in the Sussex County Court to testify in several cases concerning land ownership. At first, the court was reluctant to accept a deposition from a person of color, but after Johnson declared that he was Christian and understood the significance of an oath, his testimony was accepted. In 1684, court records indicated the estate of Nathaniel Bradford was in the "Custody of John Johnson, the Negro." In 1704, Johnson was eighty years old and unable to care for himself. The county court ordered that fifty shillings of public money be spent for "keeping and maintaining John Johnson an old free Negro."

John Johnson lived alongside Africans who were slaves. No one knows for certain when the first slave arrived in southern Delaware. On June 13, 1682, William Clark agreed to buy a servant named Black Will. The bill of sale suggested that Will was a slave, bound for life: "Whereas William Clark did buy of Captain John Osborne of Somerset County in the province of Maryland, a Negro man called or known by the name of Black Will for and during his natural life." The next line in the bill of sale, however, stated that Clark saw Will more as an indentured servant:

> *Nevertheless, the said William Clark do*[es], *for the encouragement of the said Negro servant hereby, promise, covenant, and agree that if the said Black Will do and shall well and truly serve the said William Clark, his executors, administrators and assignees* [for] *five years from the twentieth day of May last past, the said Black Will shall be clear and free of and from any further or longer servitude or slavery.*

Whether or not Will was a slave, other colonists, black and white, made their way up the Nanticoke and brought their slaves and indentured servants with them. By the time of the American Revolution, the status of slaves was clearly defined by law. The growing Delmarva community of free people of color, however, lived in a legal world that was as murky as the dark forests around the Nanticoke.

In the early nineteenth century, Levin Thompson, a free person of color, and Patty Cannon were almost neighbors. Thompson lived east of Laurel near Trussum Pond, while Patty lived a dozen or so miles to the west. In 1794, Thompson purchased 200 acres of land that he named "Thompson's Beginning." Thompson eventually owned more than 500 acres of farmland in Little Creek Hundred and 135 acres of cypress timberland in Dagsboro Hundred. In addition to working several hundred acres of farmland and timberland, Thompson operated a gristmill and a sawmill at the head of

Trussum Pond, where Levin Thompson had his mills and led a community of free people of color. *Photo by Michael Morgan.*

Trussum Pond. He also owned several spinning wheels and a loom that produced two hundred yards of linen and sixty yards of woolen cloth a month. Thompson earned interest on the capital that he had accumulated by lending money to others, including to local white farmers. For some of his enterprises, Thompson formed partnerships with white neighbors who were able to assist him through the tangled legal network that restricted blacks. In addition, one of Thompson's neighbors was Judge Isaac Cooper, an important political leader in Sussex County, who may have served as his mentor.

Thompson employed numerous free African Americans, and many of his workers purchased the freedom of their relatives. The practice of free African Americans purchasing the freedom of family members was not uncommon in Sussex County. Skilled African Americans, free and slave, took in outside work in an effort to generate enough money to buy the freedom of a relative or friend.

Thompson's workers were among some of Patty Cannon's neighbors to buy their freedom. For many centuries, ferrous material had been precipitating from the water of the Nanticoke and other waterways in the central part of the Delmarva Peninsula. The iron-laden matter settled to the bottom of these creeks and streams to accumulate into a boggy iron ore. In the eighteenth century, Colonel Joseph Vaughan built a furnace in Sussex County, near Concord, on Deep Creek, a tributary of the Nanticoke. A few years later, Vaughn added a forge on the river. Also in operation during Patty's time were the Pine Grove Furnace, near Concord; the Unity Forge on the Nanticoke River; a forge operated by Josiah Polk on the south side of Broad Creek near Laurel; and a forge established by John Collins (a future governor of Delaware), established on Gravelly Branch north of Seaford. Farther east near the Indian River, William Waples and others opened a blast furnace and foundry at Millsboro. In Maryland, the Nassawango Ironworks was in operation west of Snow Hill on a tributary of the Pocomoke River.

The Nassawango Ironworks before they were restored. Furnaces and forges once were common in the central Delmarva area. People of color were employed at these ironworks in skilled positions that enabled some of them to earn money to purchase their own freedom and the freedom of their relatives. *Photograph courtesy of the Julia A. Purnell Museum.*

Colonial iron-making required men with skill, strong backs and steady determination. The bog ore needed to be wrestled from the ground and carted across primitive roads of Delmarva to a furnace, where charcoal provided the heat needed to smelt the raw ore into pig iron. The ironworks of southern Delaware were fueled by charcoal that was produced in a space that had been cleared in the forest. The process of turning raw timber into charcoal began with the felling of trees, cutting of timber into manageable pieces and stacking the pieces into a rough conical mound that was covered with a blanket of pine needles and coated with earth. The wood inside the mound was lit; and the smoldering pile of timber took two to four weeks to char. During that time, the burning mound of timber had to be tended twenty-four hours a day. The "burners," as they were known, occasionally poked air holes in the burning pile so that they could see the color of the smoke, which indicated how the charring was progressing. The burners also were alert to cover hot spots that could reduce the timber to ashes.

All of these tasks required a skilled workforce, and slaves were used in all areas of the iron-making process. The skills that these slaves acquired made them especially valuable to their masters, who sometimes allowed them to take in extra work and keep some of the money that they earned. In addition to Levin Thompson's workers, many ironworking slaves used these funds to purchase their freedom and the freedom of their family members.

Two decades after Levin Thompson purchased his first acreage in southern Delaware, the number of free African Americans in Sussex County increased significantly, and Thompson's Beginning proved to be a thriving community of free workers who made Levin Thompson one of the richest men in that part of the Delmarva Peninsula.

The lofty principles of the American Revolution coincided with the beginning of the abolitionist movement in Delaware and led to an increase in the number of masters who chose to manumit (free) their slaves. In addition, laws were passed to make it illegal to bring slaves into Delaware and to transport them out of the state. By the time that Patty Cannon had begun her criminal career, the majority of the people of color in Delaware were free, and Maryland's free black population was growing. Nonetheless, slavery remained thoroughly entrenched in both states, and free African Americans faced a thicket of laws and customs designed to keep them in check.

Despite these laws, the white population had a deeply rooted fear that free people of color would incite slaves to revolt. In 1797, wealthy African American entrepreneur and sea captain Paul Cuffee sailed up the Nanticoke River and docked at Vienna. Cuffee's ship was crewed by black sailors, and his arrival set off a panic. Cuffee recalled in his memoirs, "The white inhabitants were stuck with apprehension of the injurious effects which such circumstances would have on the minds of their slaves, suspecting that [Cuffee] wished secretly to kindle the spirit of rebellion and excite a destructive revolt among them." The town's residents, however, quickly changed their opinion: "In a few days the inimical association vanished, and the inhabitants treated him and his crew with respect and even kindness. Many of the principal people visited his vessel, and in consequence of the pressing invitation of one them, Paul dined with his family in the town."

The lingering fear of what free blacks would do was at the root of much of the legislation passed restricting the rights of free people of color. In Delaware, any free black who was unable to pay a debt could be sold as a slave. Although the experiences of John Johnson and Levin Thompson indicated that there had been some progress, free people of color lived a murky legal existence, and they became prime targets for Patty Cannon.

"Indulgent to Criminality"

When Patty, Brereton and the two Griffith brothers set out after Ridgell, they took a circuitous route so as not to alert the slave-trader, to avoid the authorities and to evade a new threat to the success of their ambush: the British. Patty was born at about the time of the American Revolution, and in her formative years, the colonies won their independence. She was a grown woman in 1787, when the federal Constitution was written. The Constitution recognized slavery, and it prohibited outlawing the African slave trade for twenty years. In 1807, however, it did just that by passing a law that beginning in 1808, it would "not be lawful to import or bring into the United States or the territories thereof from any foreign kingdom, place or country any negro, mulatto, or person of color, with intent to hold, sell or dispose of such as a slave." The law also provided stiff penalties for anyone caught importing slaves. Outlawing the importation of slaves was akin to stopping the importation of foreign oil in the twentieth century. With the supply cut off and the continued demand for slaves, especially in the expanding South, the prices of slaves began to rise. In contrast to in the South, the demand for Delaware slaves was declining. Although Delaware banned the exportation of slaves, that law was easily evaded.

When Ridgell, looking for slaves at bargain prices, arrived at Patty Cannon's house for small talk and business, the United States was at war with Great Britain. Of all of the many causes of the War of 1812, impressment of American sailors was perhaps the most important. Locked into a titanic struggle with Napoleon Bonaparte, the British Royal Navy was chronically short of sailors, and under British law, any Englishman could be forced to serve in the navy. In the early eighteenth century, British ships routinely stopped American vessels and impressed sailors who could not prove that they were American citizens. Although American sailors carried papers to verify their citizenship, these papers were often ignored, and the unfortunate sailors were hauled away to serve an indefinite sentence aboard the king's ships, where officers ruled their crews as Southern overseers ruled their slaves. The food was poor, pay was often delayed and punishments were brutal. Petty infractions could earn a sailor a flogging of twelve lashes with the cat-o'-nine-tails made of a stiff handle and nine pieces of line. A flogging of seventy-two lashes was not unusual.

When Patty and her cohorts ambushed Ridgell, the War of 1812 was not going well for the Americans. The British Navy regularly sailed into the Chesapeake and Delaware bays, harassing vessels and threatening shore communities. Charles Ball, a contemporary of Patty's, wrote graphically about his experiences as a slave and saw the hazards of sailing on the Nanticoke firsthand. During 1813, British warships entered Chesapeake Bay and took aboard a number of fugitive slaves. An emissary was dispatched to the British ships to negotiate the return of the runaway slaves. The emissary was accompanied by Charles Ball, who was born a slave in Maryland, acquired his freedom, was kidnapped back into slavery and escaped again. While on the British warship, Ball reported, "One day a small schooner was seen standing out of the mouth of the Nanticoke River, and beating up the bay." The schooner, captained by its owner and containing a cargo of corn and several passengers, was captured by the British, and "after her cargo had been removed, she was burned in view of her owner, who seemed much affected at the sight, and said that it was all the property he owned in the world, and that his wife and children were now beggars."

When Ridgell's carriage disappeared down the road, Patty Cannon and her gang were not thinking of the war, the British or impressed sailors. The British may have intercepted vessels at the mouth of the Nanticoke, but they did not venture up the river as far as Cannon's Ferry. What was important to Patty and her gang was that the ambush had failed to get the slave trader's money. They also knew that they had murdered a man and failed to prevent the escape of a prime witness. When Ridgell and his companion reached Laurel, they reported the circumstances surrounding the attempted robbery and murder: how the two men had enjoyed their stay at Patty's house, that they disclosed their desire to buy slaves and how they foolishly divulged that they carried a large sum of money. In the confusion of ambush and gunfire, the surviving trader may not have had a good look at his attackers, but the suspicion was strong that the Cannon gang was at work. The authorities needed to get one of the suspected assailants to talk, and Jesse Griffith did.

Jesse and his brother John were from a humble Sussex County family. In 1820, the *Easton Gazette and Eastern Shore Intelligencer* reported that their father

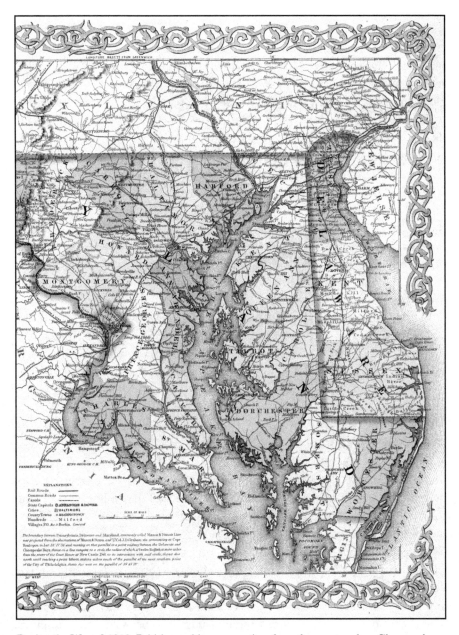

During the War of 1812, British warships were active along the coast and on Chesapeake and Delaware Bays, waters that were normally sailed by Patty and her gang. *Courtesy of the Delaware Public Archives.*

died when they were young, and their mother was said to be "indulgent to criminality" and brought the two boys "up in idleness." Jesse was allowed "the practice of those things which idleness generally lead to." When he became a man, Jesse drifted from job to job. The *Easton Gazette and Eastern Shore Intelligencer* also remarked, "He seems not to have entered upon any constant employment for living, yet he could do as good a day's work as most men, and followed different occupations at different times and in different places." Jesse's only constant employment, if it could be called that, was when he and brother, John, joined Harry Brereton and Patty Cannon's gang of crooks.

When confronted by the Sussex County authorities, Jesse sang like a bird on a holiday. He told how the Cannon gang set up the phony sale so that they could ambush the slave traders on the road to Laurel. He described how he, his brother and Brereton circled through the back roads and laid brush in the road to stop the traders' carriage. He described the failed ambush and supplied enough details to arrest his brother and Brereton, who were taken to the courthouse in Georgetown.

In 1813, the county seat of Georgetown was only two decades old. Laid in 1792 to provide a more central location for the county government, the streets of Georgetown were laid out in a simple grid pattern with a town square in the center. In the middle of the square was a circular path to facilitate traffic, of which there was little, and around the square stood the architecture of government: courthouse, jail, whipping post and pillory. The courthouse was a two-story wooden frame building that matched the old courthouse in Lewes, the former county seat. In 1798, the original jail was augmented by a stout, two-story brick addition that contained three cells on each of its two floors, making it the most substantial building in a town dominated by wooden frame dwellings. In addition, the whipping post and pillory were taken down from Lewes and transported to Georgetown, where they were set up near the courthouse.

After their arrest, Griffith and Brereton were brought to the courthouse, where they were tried, found guilty of murder and sentenced to hang. While they awaited their execution in the brick jail, simple gallows were constructed, and people began to flood into Georgetown from the surrounding area. The executions of Griffith and Brereton may have been the first hangings in Georgetown's short history. So many people crowded into town in anticipation of the hangings that the county authorities began to worry that things might get out of hand.

As the execution day approached in Georgetown, along the coast, a British flotilla anchored off Lewes and demanded provisions. The citizens

Georgetown, Delaware, in the middle of the nineteenth century. The courthouse, jail, pillory and stocks bordered on the square in the middle of town. *Courtesy of the Delaware Public Archives.*

refused, and on April 6 and 7, the British subjected the town to a severe bombardment. Daniel Rodney, prominent Lewes merchant and politician, noted in his journal on April 6, 1813, "The cannoned then commenced and continued till 10—their shot pitched beyond the town and did but little damage—firing ceased until daylight." The next day the bombardment continued, but the town refused to surrender. Having failed to pound Lewes into submission, the British sailed away to look for provisions elsewhere.

In the midst of the encounter with the British, a message was received from the county officials in Georgetown requesting assistance controlling the crowd that was assembling for the execution of Griffith and Brereton.

Three days after the bombardment of Lewes, Rodney noted in his journal, "Col. Davis, at the sheriff's request, detached Captain Kollock and 20 men to attend the execution of Henry Brereton and [John] Griffin [*sic*] on Tuesday at Georgetown for the murder of Ridgell of Carolina." Kollock's detachment was able to keep things in check, and on April 13, Rodney reported, "Brereton and Griffin [*sic*] were hanged this day at Georgetown about 12 o'clock. A great concourse of people attended from this and adjoining counties."

Although he implicated his brother, it is not known what Jesse Griffith said of Patty Cannon's role in the ambush. It is also not known what the surviving slave trader said of her involvement. It was night, she was dressed in men's clothing at the time and the trader may not have realized that she was there. At any rate, the authorities chose not prosecute her, and having abandoned Patty's gang, Jesse Griffith resumed his former life as a drifter. In 1820, the *Easton Gazette and Eastern Shore Intelligencer* commented, "This affair was a broad, black stain on the already spotted characters of poor Jesse, a stain which he would never wipe off but with his own blood." Shunned by the public for his criminal behavior, and an outcast among outlaws for betraying his own brother and Brereton, Griffith lived in shacks on the Nanticoke upstream from Vienna, sometimes in Maryland and sometimes in Delaware. He was blamed for robbing smokehouses, barns and other outbuildings, and from time to time, gangs of men would gather to drive him away and demolish his hut. Despite his treatment, "he seemed at any rate to possess the noble quality of bearing almost insuperable difficulties with fortitude and courage."

Jesse erected a cabin on an island in Maryland on a half acre of land in the Nanticoke River near a large marshy area. Jesse's wife had left him, and he took up with Betsey Askridge, whose mother moved in with him, and reportedly "perhaps a female or two besides." One day, Griffith and a man named McOlister went into the swamp to cut wood when the two got into an argument. Griffith struck McOlister and threatened to "make beef of his oxen."

McOlister complained to the sheriff, but the sheriff refused to arrest Griffith, saying, "An attempt of that kind would be attended with serious consequences." A man named Kirkley volunteered to serve as a deputy, was sworn in and went off with the warrant to arrest "the terror of the neighborhood." After one or two failures, Kirkley gathered a posse of men with firearms and a man named Hinson Tull, who had only a sword.

On a December night in 1818, the posse approached the crude cabin, where Griffith lay sick in bed with the measles. Kirkley's posse surrounded the house, and Tull pushed open the door. From his bed, Griffith called out,

"Who's there?" and Tull answered, "Nobody shall hurt you, but Kirkley and his men have come to take you." Meanwhile, some of Kirkley's men, including Jim LeCompte, began to rip the planks from Griffith's cabin. After Griffith told Tull to get out, a shot was fired, and Tull fell dead. Others in the posse rushed into the cabin, and Griffith was arrested. At his trial, Griffith pled not guilty, contending that LeCompt had fired the shot through an opening in the planks that killed Tull. Asked why LeCompt would shoot Tull, Griffith said, "Jim LeCaompt was drunk, and when he is drunk he is crazy and no doubt he thought it was me trying to escape."

Griffith was found guilty and sentenced to be hanged. At 11:00 a.m. on August 16, 1820, the condemned man was brought out of Cambridge jail dressed in his burial shroud. Taking a seat on a cart, which was followed by several ministers, Jesse Griffith began the slow procession to the place of execution. When he reached the gallows, Griffith was asked by the sheriff if he had any final words. After a short pause, he struggled to his feet and in a faint voice, professed his belief that God would save his soul. Griffith went on to say, "As to the crime for which I am to die, God knows I am innocent of it—I never hurt a hair on his head, nor do I tell who it was that did, through malice or ill will; but it was James LeCompte who killed the man, and I have now to die for his fault."

After Griffith warned young people against drunkenness and bad company, the ministers began singing the solemn hymn "Judgment":

> And must I be to judgment brought,
> To answer on that day,
> For every wicked, idle thought,
> And every word I say?
>
> Yes, every secret of my heart
> Shall shortly be made known,
> And I receive my just desert
> For all that I have done.

After one of the ministers said a few words, the sheriff asked, "Ready?" The trap was sprung, and Jesse Griffith was, as the *Easton Gazette* put it, "launched into eternity."

Chapter 2
A Career of Crime

THE INFAMOUS TRAFFIC

For Patty, there were lessons to be learned from the failed ambush on the slave trader Ridgell. An attack on white people, especially ones with money and connections, was risky, and if it failed, all of the resources of the law could be brought to bear on Patty and her gang. In the future, Patty would be careful to make sure that there were no witnesses, and she took pains to thoroughly dispose of any dead bodies.

A few years after the War of 1812 ended, a slave trader arrived at Patty's house. Like Ridgell, this man had cash, $15,000, with which to buy slaves. Here was a target that Patty found too tempting to resist, and she would not repeat the errors of the murder of Ridgell. While the slave trader was eating supper, she nonchalantly walked behind him and stabbed him in the back, killing him. With the dead man's bloody body slumped over the table, other travelers arrived. Before they entered the house, Patty threw the dead man onto the table with the dishes, wrapped dishes and corpse in the tablecloth and dumped the bundle into a blue box. She then turned on her feminine charms and entertained the travelers until they left. Patty, along with the Johnson brothers, then carried the dead man's body outside the house. Selecting a burial plot beneath a small pile of rubbish, they dug a shallow grave and laid the murdered man to rest.

Killing a white slave trader and disposing of the corpse left few clues, but kidnapping a slave had its hazards. A slave was property owned by a white master who could summon the legal apparatus against the thief. On the other hand, free people of color were inviting targets. Slave droves, with ten or twenty slaves in chains, were a common sight on Delmarva, and few people would question the legality of those in chains. In addition, kidnappers were careful to keep their victims from conversing with strangers, and this allowed Patty's gang to march their captives in shackles in daylight from Patty's house and Johnson's Tavern to the Nanticoke River without fear of attracting undue attention.

Some free African Americans on Delmarva, like those in Levin Thompson's community near Trussum Pond or those employed at the ironworks in the boggy areas of Maryland and Delaware, had influential white friends who might intercept kidnap victims before they could be shipped South. On the other hand, African Americans, either free or slave, in Baltimore, Wilmington and Philadelphia made more inviting targets who could be abducted and transported to Patty Cannon's house, which was not only located on the border between Delaware and Maryland but also the building sat just a few hundred yards from the dividing line of Maryland's Dorchester and Caroline Counties. The second story of Patty's house contained two rooms that were not connected. Each of these rooms formed a cell that was accessible by a separate staircase. The unique arrangement of these two rooms made them ideal for holding kidnap victims.

Stealthy by nature, criminal gangs leave few records of their nefarious activities and fewer traces of their informal command structure. Those around Patty were a loose collection of malcontents who came and went as they were arrested, killed or moved on to other dubious ventures. Joe Johnson, an experienced kidnapper, was physically intimidating, six foot tall, mean and fearless. Johnson maintained a tavern in what became known as Johnson's Crossroads, where the road leading from Cannon's Ferry to Federalsburg, Maryland, intersected with the road from Seaford to Hurlock, Maryland. Situated a short distance from Patty's house, the tavern next to the Maryland-Delaware border was on the road to Cannon's Ferry. With easy access to the Nanticoke River, the victims collected at Patty's house cold be added to those at the tavern and shipped down the river to Southern ports, where they could be sold for handsome profits.

Although Joe Johnson and his brother, Ebenezer, would gain substantial notoriety, Patty remained the focus of the gang that included Thomas Collins, John Purnell and Cyrus James. Unlike Collins and Purnell, Cyrus

James was indentured to Patty when he was seven years old. There has been some debate over whether James was white or black, but the consensus is that he was white. In the nineteenth century, when referring to a person of color, the practice was to indicate that fact by saying that they were Negro, black, mulatto or some other word that showed that they were not white. Cyrus James was not identified as such. While other members of the gang came and went, James remained with Patty and witnessed many of her most horrendous crimes. She was the one constant in the kidnapping, thieving, murdering group of criminals that thrived on the Delaware-Maryland border during the first three decades of the nineteenth century. Before her emergence, there was no gang, and after her death, the gang dissolved. Although no contemporary letter, diary or newspaper detailed her role, the documents that were generated within a few years of her death cast her as the leader of the gang. Avoiding the law by using her feminine wiles and adroitly moving back and forth across the Maryland-Delaware border, she pursued her criminal career for over a decade and a half.

On another occasion, three members of Patty's gang were hunting for a likely kidnap victim. Late in the evening, one of the gang members decoyed a light-skinned indentured servant into thinking that he was going on a possum hunt. When the victim was far enough away from his house so that his cries for help could not be heard, the other two members of Patty's gang, armed with pistols, rushed him, tied him with ropes and led him away. As they traveled, two of the kidnappers, with theirs pistols at the ready, walked on either side of the captured servant and threatened to shoot if he made any cry for help.

After hiking fifteen or twenty miles through the fields and forests of southern Delaware, he was placed aboard a small carriage that carried him to Johnson's Tavern. After a brief stay at the tavern, he was transported down the Nanticoke and across the Chesapeake Bay. While near Annapolis, the captive indentured servant was able to tell a black woman that he was free, but when his guard overheard him, the guard threatened to shoot him if he caught him telling anybody else that he was free. Finally, the kidnapped servant arrived in Washington and was taken to a three-story brick tavern on F Street, where he was chained in the attic with several more victims of Patty's gang. One of these was a light-skinned man, about twenty-one years of age, who was manacled with strong U-shaped loops around his wrists, connected by a strong iron bolt. On the shelf, over the fireplace, lay a pair of heavy rough harnesses with which, he said, his legs had been fettered. The harness resembled horse fetters with locks, connected by a strong new tug chain, with a loose end two or three feet long.

As described by the abolitionist Jesse Torrey, a free family of color was surprised by Patty Cannon's gang of kidnappers and dragged away. From *A Portraiture of Domestic Slavery in the United States.*

In the tavern attic, there was also a young black woman and an infant who were born free. She lived in Delaware with her husband and worked as a servant. When her husband passed away, the kidnappers saw an opportunity to seize her. The woman lived in her employer's house and slept on a small bed in the kitchen. A few days after her husband's death, the owner of the house, his brother and three members of Patty's gang came into the kitchen and dragged her from her bed. After looping a noose around her neck, they attempted to blindfold her. While one of the kidnappers was trying to tie a cloth over her eyes, she bit his cheek and tore off a piece of it. Taking a large wooden stick, one of the men struck her head several times, opening a deep bloody gash.

As the woman, now covered with blood, and the men struggled, she screamed for help, and the owner of the house shouted, "Choke the damned bitch! Don't let her halloo—she'll scare my wife!"

The woman was finally subdued, and she and her baby were carried to a small carriage. With a noose around her neck and two kidnappers on horseback on either side of the vehicle, she was driven to Johnson's Tavern, where a slave trader arrived to purchase the woman. While her captors and the slave trader were negotiating, the trader asked her who her master was.

She said that she had none, and Patty's henchmen immediately ushered the slave trader into another room, where the deal was concluded.

The slave trader brought the woman and her child to Washington, and along the way he confessed that he thought she might have some claim to freedom. He would have taken her back, he said, but the man who had sold her was probably gone. He asked her not to say anything about being free, but she refused, and when she was offered for sale to several buyers, they refused when they heard that she might be free. The slave trader brought her to a tavern on F Street, where she was chained in the attic. The wound in her head healed, leaving a large scar on her forehead. The slave trader, who needed enough people to make a drove for Georgia, returned to the Eastern Shore, where he likely paid another visit to Johnson's Tavern or Patty Cannon's house. According to Jesse Torrey, an abolitionist who investigated the kidnappings at the time, when slave traders with abundant cash arrived, they were like "beasts of prey…extending their ravages, generally attended with bloodshed and sometimes murder, and spreading terror and consternation amongst both freemen and slaves throughout the sandy regions form the western to the eastern shores. These 'two-legged featherless animals' or human blood-hounds, when overtaken (rarely) by messengers of the law, are generally found armed with instruments of death, sometimes with pistols with latent spring daggers attached to them!"

Also in the tavern attic with Patty's kidnapped victims was a woman whose battered body lay on a bed covered with a blood-spotted, white woolen blanket. Unlike the kidnapped victims, the woman was a legal slave who lived near Bladensburg, Maryland, with her husband. She said, "They brought me away with two of my children, and wouldn't let me see my husband—they didn't sell my husband, and I didn't want to go." Distraught with the prospect of being sold South, she devised a plan to escape.

People of color who knew that they were being sold to a Southern slave plantation were driven to desperate measures. Charles Ball, the African American who described the British efforts to suppress the trade on the Chesapeake and the Nanticoke, also left a graphic depiction of the realities of slavery. According to Ball, "If a negro is wronged, there is no one to whom he can complain—if suffering for want of the coarsest food, he dare not steal—if flogged till the flesh falls from his bones, he must not murmur—and if compelled to perform his daily toil in an iron collar, no expression of resentment must escape his lips."

In addition to the floggings, Ball witnessed an insidious torture inflicted upon slaves known as the punishment of the pump: a female house servant who had displeased her master was stripped naked and tied to a post that stood just under the stream of water from the pump spout. A young man was then ordered to pump water upon the head and shoulders of the victim. After a minute under the waterfall from the pump, the woman began to cry and scream. Writhing in pain, under the cascade of water, Ball explained,

> *When the water first strikes the head and the arms, it is not at all painful; but in a short time it produces the sensation that is felt when heavy blows are inflicted with large rods, of the size of a man's finger. This perception becomes more and more painful, until the skull bone and shoulder blades appear to be broken in pieces. Finally, all the faculties become oppressed; breathing becomes more and more difficult; until the eyesight become dim and animation ceases. The punishment is, in fact, a temporary murder.*

After the punishment, the victim would be put into a bed and covered with warm blankets. After a day or two, the effects of the torture would wear off, and the slave returned to work.

Kidnapped slaves who were taken to the South were far from home and family and friends who could come to their aid. After he was kidnapped, Ball wrote, "I was far from the place of my nativity, in a land of strangers, with no one to care for me, beyond the care that master bestows upon his ox; with all future life, one long, waste, barren desert, of cheerless, hopeless, lifeless slavery; to be varied only by the pangs of hunger and the stings of the lash."

In addition to facing all of these horrors, a young female who was deemed to be a "fancy girl" could be used at her master's pleasure, and it is not surprising that African Americans chose suicide over slavery. As Ball wrote, "What is life worth, amidst hunger, nakedness and excessive toil, under the continually uplifted lash?" Shortly after the War of 1812, there were a number of reports of people of color attempting suicide rather than be taken to the plantations of the South. A woman in Washington who learned that she had been sold to the Southern slave market cut her own throat, and a female slave who had been sold in Maryland with her child cut the throats of both her child and herself. In Philadelphia, an African American youth cut his throat when he suspected that he would be sold to Southerners.

The woman lying in the bed in the tavern attic had been left unchained, and on the evening of December 19, 1815, she attempted to escape by jumping out the window of the three-story building. The woman landed in a crumpled heap with her back and both arms broken between the elbows and wrists. Unable to stand, she lay moaning loudly in the street. Her struggling groans awoke the mayor of Washington, James H. Blake, who lived nearby. Blake happened to be a medical doctor, who rushed to her aid. He set the broken bones in her arms, but he could do little for her crushed spine. The mayor saw that she was returned to the tavern, where she was abandoned by the slave traders who took the woman's two children to the Carolinas. The traders left her in the possession of the tavern-keeper as compensation for taking care of her.

Reports of kidnapped people of color by Patty's gang reached the abolitionist Jesse Torrey, who traveled across Delaware into Maryland to Washington, D.C., to investigate the veracity of these rumors. Torrey visited the tavern on F Street, where he discovered the woman who had jumped from the window and several African Americans manacled in the attic. He asked the woman whether she was sleep-walking and accidently fell out of the garret window. The woman replied, "No, no more than I am now." He then asked her why she jumped from the window, and she answered, "I was so confused and distracted that I didn't know hardly what I was about—but I didn't want to go, and I jumped out of the window."

Torrey believed that the woman would never walk again and had little hope of ever seeing her children, who had been dispersed to parts unknown. Torrey also interviewed the three others who were being held in the attic, and he learned that they had been kidnapped in Delaware by Patty's gang. When he finished his investigation, Torrey published his findings in *A Portraiture of Domestic Slavery in the United States*, which was released in 1817. In addition to documenting crimes of Patty Cannon's gang, Torrey reported that William B. Cooper, a Laurel native and at the time a member of the United States House of Representatives, told him that the fear of being abducted by kidnappers was so great that he was afraid to send his servants out in the evening. Torrey also discovered that people of color were afraid to go to Georgetown for fear of being caught on the road by kidnappers. In his book, Torrey did not refer to Patty Cannon and Jesse Johnson by name, but his description of the tavern "near the dividing line of Maryland and Delaware" gave authorities a clear picture of what was happening in Patty's house and Johnson's Tavern.

After Torrey heard the stories of the captives in the attic, he went across the bay to the Delmarva Peninsula and traveled to Wilmington, Lewes and Georgetown. He discovered, as a well-heeled resident of Delaware put it, "as vile a banditti as ever were permitted to disturb the peace of society… Their gang is numerous, daring—full of money, etc." He arrived back in Washington with enough evidence to convince a court to free those who had been kidnapped.

Above: Jesse Torrey interviewing the people of color held prisoner in the attic of a tavern on F Street in Washington, D.C. The woman who jumped from the attic window lies near the wall. From *A Portraiture of Domestic Slavery in the United States.*

Opposite: The woman who jumped from a window in a tavern attic in Washington, D.C., attracted so much notice that the abolitionist Jesse Torrey traveled from Philadelphia to the nation's capital to investigate the truth of the incident. From *A Portraiture of Domestic Slavery in the United States.*

Torrey concluded:

> *From the best information that I have had opportunities to collect, in travelling by various routes through the states of Delaware and Maryland, and from statements of an ingenious trader exclusively, (as I believe,) in lawful slaves, I am fully convinced that there are, at this time, within the jurisdiction of the United States, several thousands of legally free people of color, toiling under the yoke of involuntary servitude, and transmitting the same fate to their posterity!*

TELLTALE SCARS

Patty's kidnapping gang continued to extend their range and the complexity of their abductions. Slaves, black indentured servants and free people of

Thirty Dollars Reward.

RAN away from the subscriber, living at the Upper ferry on South River, in Anne-Arundel county, on Wednesday the 21st ult. a negro man named CHARLES, about twenty-two or twenty-three years old, five feet seven inches high, of a yellowish complexion, the inside of one of his ears has a knot occasioned by a fall, his foreteeth are very broad, has a very broad foot and narrow heel; had on when he went away a gre coaten, striped waist-coat, and ofnabrig troufers, and had other cloaths in a bundle which are unknown. He was feen near the city of Baltimore a few days after he went off.

Whoever takes up and fecures the faid negro in any gaol, fo that I get him again, fhall receive the above reward. I hereby forewarn all perfons from employing or harbouring him.

Oct. 6, 1803.

25   THOMAS PINDLE.

This advertisement for a fugitive slave describes what he was wearing when he left his master's Maryland farm and stated that "the inside of one of his ears has a knot occasioned by a fall." From the *Maryland Gazette*, July 5, 1804.

color often worked closely with their white masters, but their masters often could only identify them from distinctive scars or body blemishes. Newspaper advertisements for runaways almost always featured the clothes the fugitive had on when he left and a physical description that included his height, misshaped teeth, a knot from a poorly healed broken bone and scars and blemishes that might be an area of the skin that was whiter than the rest of the skin or a pit from smallpox.

In 1829, Mahala Purnell ran away from a farm in Worcester County, Maryland. When Purnell's master, a man named Bowen, discovered that Mahala and her husband had fled, he immediately set out to capture the two slaves. After an extensive but fruitless search that extended from Maryland well into Delaware, Bowen returned to Maryland. Twenty-two years later in

Philadelphia, several men came to the home of Euphemia Williams. Amid cries by one of her children of "They've got my mother! They've got my mother!" the men dragged the mother of six children away. "For God's sake, save me!" Williams shouted, but to no avail. The men hustled Euphemia off to the marshal's office and charged her with being the fugitive slave Mahala Purnell. She was taken to the loft of Independence Hall to await a hearing to be held the next day. At the hearing, Bowen identified Euphemia Williams as Mahala Purnell. Three other witnesses paraded to the witness stand, and they verified Bowen's testimony that Euphemia was Bowen's slave Mahala. One witness's testimony was typical: "If you could see the rest of the family, you could pick her out yourself...not by any particular mark...I never saw any marks upon her."

The lawyers defending Euphemia Williams maintained that she was not Mahala Purnell, and they called Sarah Gayly to testify. Gayly maintained that she knew Williams when they were both young. According to Gayly, "I have not seen her since 1826, until I saw her here in the courtroom; I recognized her when I first saw her here without anybody pointing her out, and she recognized me."

At this point, it was Gayly's testimony against the four witnesses who swore that Euphemia was a runaway slave, but then she added: "I have reason to know her, because she has the same sort of a scar on her forehead that I have; we used to make fun of each other about the marks." The judge asked the defendant to come forward, and as she approached the judge, she removed her headscarf to reveal a scar that collaborated Gayly's testimony. The judge immediately dismissed the case and declared Euphemia Williams free.

Kidnappers knew a telltale scar or blemish carried considerable weight as evidence in court, and they used this knowledge to their advantage. After a potential victim was identified, some kidnappers employed an accomplice, sometimes a person of color, who became friendly with the unsuspecting target. After spending a little time together, the accomplice learned whatever identifying scars or blemish the victim had. The kidnappers would then claim that the target was their runaway slave, who was then hauled before a magistrate. At the hearing, the kidnappers would describe the marks on the victim's body, and the magistrate would award them custody of the unfortunate person of color, who would be whisked away to the South before anyone could discover the truth.

The use of accomplices was particularly valuable as Patty's gang extended their operations beyond the Nanticoke River. In 1816, John Milner was in cahoots with the gang when he hired Abram Luomony, a free person of color, to be part of the crew of the *Betsy*, a small sailing vessel engaged in the coastal trade. The *Betsy* was sailing near the mouth of the Broadkill, a short distance from the town of Lewes. As the vessel approached a bridge, Joe Johnson leapt aboard. Johnson and Milner beat, robbed and tied up Luomony. Led by Johnson and aided by William Miller, another member of the *Betsy*'s crew, the kidnappers took their victim ashore.

Once on land, Johnson loaded Luomony aboard a carriage for the trip across southern Delaware to Jesse Cannon's house. After three days of confinement, Luomony slipped out of his restraints and escaped. He contacted some Delaware abolitionists, who helped him reach Philadelphia, where information about his abduction was turned over to the authorities.

Armed with this information, the authorities began to close in on Patty's gang, who pursued their kidnappings unabated. Jesse Cannon brazenly abducted John Parker, a free black, near Georgetown, Delaware. It was risky kidnapping someone close to home, but neither Jesse nor Patty could resist an easy target. On several occasions, when Patty encountered a person of color along the road, she is said to have knocked down her victims, tied them up, put them into a cart and carried them over to Johnson's Tavern. In this manner, Parker was quickly transported and sold to an owner in Annapolis. Parker and a woman who had been kidnapped along with her children ended up with the same owner. John Parker and the woman were able to successfully sue for their freedom. Because the slave owners were unaware that they had purchased kidnapped slaves, they were not charged, and the evidence against Jesse Cannon was not substantial enough to charge him with a crime. The evidence was building, however, that Joe Johnson, Jesse Cannon and his wife, Patty, were engaged in an illicit trade of blacks.

In 1819, Sarah Hagerman, a young, free black woman from Philadelphia, was kidnapped and sold to Jesse Cannon, who was believed to be living on the Maryland side of the border. Hagerman's abduction, however, came to the attention of John H. Willis of the Pennsylvania Abolition Society, and he went to Maryland and met with a local sheriff, who told him that Cannon lived on the Delaware side of the border. The sheriff referred Willis to Anthony Wheatley, a member of the Maryland Abolition Society. Wheatley was well aware of Cannon's activities, stealing and buying African Americans, slave and free. Wheatley told Willis to meet with one of Cannon's neighbors, Hatfield Wright, who was sympathetic to the plight of African Americans.

When Willis and Wright met, they devised a plan to determine whether Sarah Hagerman was being held in the dark recesses of Cannon's home.

On several occasions, Patty Cannon and Joe Johnson kidnapped people of color when they encountered them alone on an isolated stretch of road. From *A Portraiture of Domestic Slavery in the United States.*

For five dollars, they hired a man to go to the Cannon house, pretending to be in the market for a slave. Cannon allowed the man inside to inspect the people that he had in chains. He spotted Hagerman among the slaves and reported to Willis and Wright that the kidnapped victim was there. After some difficulties, the two men received a warrant to search Cannon's house. The sheriff expressed concern that this was no easy task, as Joe Johnson might be in the house and that he was known to be a violent and desperate man. After recruiting several others to help, the posse arrived at Cannon's house in the evening and split into two groups. One covered the back of the house, and the other approached the house from the front. Two young black women were at the front of the house, but neither one was Sarah Hagerman. Joe Johnson, as feared, came out of the house and declared that the warrant had expired at sunset and he intended to shoot anyone who might try to enter the house. The sheriff replied that the posse had arrived before dark and the warrant was valid. Jesse Cannon, also armed, appeared. The standoff ended when Johnson and Cannon decided to let the sheriff enter the building, provided that he did not speak to anyone inside.

When the sheriff and Willis went into the building, they went up into a large attic where the five young black women were manacled. None of the women, however, was Hagerman. Frustrated, the sheriff began to search the outbuilding, where he discovered two drunken African Americans, who seemed to be enjoying their liquor. The sheriff was forced to conclude that the man sent before them was mistaken that he had seen Hagerman or that Cannon and Johnson had grown suspicious and spirited her away. Despite this close call, Patty and her gang continued their abductions.

THE SOFT PART OF THE EARS TO BE CUT OFF

In the course of the failed attempt to rescue Sarah Hagerman, outsiders who were sympathetic to the plight of the kidnapped victims got a good look at the insides of Johnson's Tavern. The shackles and manacles in the attic could be used for lawfully restraining slaves, but they might also be an indication that a large number of slaves or kidnap victims were being held in the tavern. Patty and Joe Johnson relied on their brazen guile and the repeated failure of the authorities to file charges against them to continue their criminal activities. As the Hagerman case showed, the kidnappers, hardened by experience, used the ambiguous border to claim that they were not in the jurisdiction of whatever legal authority confronted them. In addition, Joe used his considerable physical prowess to intimidate law enforcement officials who were reluctant to confront him, unless they had abundant evidence that a crime had been committed in their jurisdiction. On the other hand, Patty relied on her feminine demeanor to conceal the fact that underneath the façade of a charming middle-aged lady was the heart of a cold-blooded killer. With the Nanticoke River providing easy access to the Chesapeake Bay, Patty's gang turned to more distant cities that contained a large number of potential victims.

Charles Ball, the African American who accompanied the emissary who attempted to retrieve the runaway slaves taken by the British, was put ashore when the negotiations failed. When the British continued operations in the Chesapeake area, Ball enlisted as a seaman and cook in Commodore Joshua Barney's flotilla that was harassing the English warships. In the summer of 1814, Barney's squadron of small ships and gunboats was forced up the Patuxent River by the British. After Barney scuttled his vessels to prevent them from being captured, he and his men marched to Bladensburg, where the American forces defending Washington, D.C., were assembling.

In the ensuing battle, most of the American troops scampered from the battlefield after firing only a few shots. Barney's flotilla men, however, made a desperate stand to prevent the British from entering Washington. Ball later recalled:

> *When we reached Bladensburg, and the flotilla men were drawn up in line, to work at their cannon, armed with their cutlasses, I volunteered to assist in working the canon that occupied the first place on the left of the Commodore...I stood at my gun, until the Commodore was shot down, when he ordered us to retreat, as I was told by the officer who commanded our gun. If the militia regiments, that lay upon our right and left, could have been brought to charge the British in close fight, as they crossed the bridge, we should have killed or taken the whole of them in a short time but the militia ran like sheep chased by dogs.*

After the Battle of Bladensburg, the British marched into Washington, burned the President's House, the Capitol and other public buildings. They then returned to their ships and set out for Baltimore, which they considered a "nest of pirates" for being the home port of so many privateers that preyed on British shipping. Ball also made his way to Baltimore, where he joined the city's large population of free people of color who were working on the town's defenses. An eyewitness noted, "White and black are all at work together. You'll see a master and his slave digging side by side. There is no distinction whatsoever."

In September 1814, the British Royal Navy failed to pound Fort McHenry into submission, the British retreated and Francis Scott Key was inspired to write the words to the "Star-Spangled Banner." The War of 1812 ended several months later, and Baltimore's trade boomed, sending ships to Europe, north along the Atlantic coast, and more importantly, south to the slave-holding states. Extending from Federal Hill to Fells Point along the northeastern shore of a branch of the Patapsco River, the Baltimore waterfront was a tangle of sailing vessels, schooners, sloops and square-riggers afloat and a motley collection of inns and saloons ashore. Baltimore was also home to slave pens, whose unfortunate captives waited for shipment to the South, and a substantial free African American population, a tempting target for Patty's gang of kidnappers. With the war over, the schooners of the Cannon-Johnson gang were free to sail down the Nanticoke and into the Chesapeake Bay unmolested, and Patty took every advantage of the peacetime conditions.

In July 1821, Captain W. Bell's small vessel cast off its moorings, lifted sail and headed past Fort McHenry and down the Patapsco. Aboard was Ebenezer

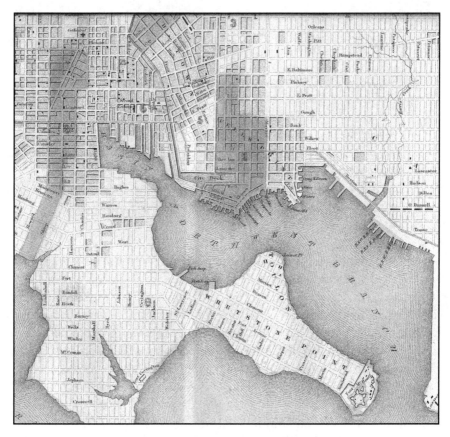

Baltimore in the early part of the nineteenth century was the third-largest city in the United States. The port facilities were located along the north bank of a branch of the Patapsco River. Fort McHenry is at the bottom right of the map. T.G. Bradford, printer, 1838. *Author's collection.*

Johnson, Joe's brother, and confined below decks was a cargo of kidnapped African Americans. On June 14, two free people of color, Jacob and Spencer Francis, brothers aged twenty and nineteen, had been seized and brought aboard the sailing vessel. Two days after the Francis brothers were taken, fifteen-year-old George Morgan, a free African American who lived with his sister in Fells Point, was captured. The same day that Morgan was seized, Ebenezer Johnson abducted ten-year-old John Dominick. On July 3, Lowel Thorpe, a twenty-three-year-old slave, was kidnapped and joined the others aboard Bell's vessel. On July 6, George Williams, nineteen years old and free, was the last kidnapped victim taken. With a cargo of half a dozen saleable captives secured in the hold, Captain Bell set sail for the Delmarva Peninsula.

Sailing vessels, such as the ones shown here, were once common on the Chesapeake Bay and the Nanticoke River. *Courtesy of the Delaware Public Archives.*

After reaching the mouth of the Patapsco, Bell turned and sailed southward. Keeping Kent Island to port and Annapolis to starboard, Bell cruised the broad expanse of the Chesapeake until he reached Tangier Sound, where he steered into the mouth of the Nanticoke River. Bell followed the winding river past Vienna until he reached the area near Cannon's Ferry. After docking, the six kidnapped men were herded like livestock to Johnson's Crossroads, where they were taken to Joe Johnson's Tavern and placed in chains.

The captives seized by Ebenezer Johnson were not enough to make a shipment to the South, but they were soon joined by others. Joe Johnson had bought three slaves: Samuel Carlisle, aged fifty-five, and two children, Nochre and Isaac Griffith. The three were owned by Nancy Griffith, who lived near Milford, Delaware. (It is not known whether Nancy was a relative of Jesse and John Griffith.) Johnson also bought the thirteen-year-old slave Henry Ingram. The four slaves were not kidnap victims, but Johnson intended to sell them out of state, which was illegal.

Joining the captives in Johnson's house were three African Americans who had been kidnapped by Lewis Duvall, one of the Cannon gang's henchmen operating in Wilmington. Duvall seized sixteen-year-old James Morris, seventeen-year-old Jacob Eveson and eleven-year-old John Todd, all free, and transported them down the Delaware Bay and eventually to Joe Johnson's house, where they joined the captives from Baltimore. Altogether, there were thirteen African Americans confined in the building. The eldest African American was fifty-five, and the next eldest were twenty-three and twenty. There were six teenagers and four children eleven and under, some in chains waiting to be sent down the Nanticoke River. At a time when an acre of land could be bought for $1, a young adult male slave was worth up to $300. The burst of activity by Joe Johnson, however, did not go unnoticed.

On July 14, Deputy Sheriffs Tindal and Johnson formed a posse to arrest Joe Johnson "on two bills of indictment found against him several years past, for kidnapping free Negroes." The posse set out for North West Fork Hundred. There had long been rumors that Johnson was involved with kidnapping and the illicit slave trade, but he had eluded the authorities by moving between Delaware and Maryland. The posse reached a point near the Maryland border at about 10:00 a.m. and surrounded the house of Jesse Cannon, where Johnson was staying. Cannon was also implicated in the kidnapping scheme. Calls for Johnson and Cannon to surrender were answered by threats by Johnson to shoot anyone who attempted to enter the house or arrest him. Johnson had second thoughts, however, when he saw that the posse had every avenue of escape blocked. After a brief negotiation, he gave himself up.

Johnson; his wife, Mary; Jesse and Patty Cannon; their son, Jesse Cannon Jr.; and a man named John Stevenson were arrested and charged with kidnapping. It appears that the evidence was strongest against Joe Johnson, who was the only one prosecuted. Helping in these efforts was a young lawyer, John Middleton Clayton. Born in 1796, Clayton was not yet twenty years old when he graduated from Yale in 1815. After establishing a legal practice in Georgetown, the heavyset Dagsboro native with sharp gray eyes, bushy sideburns and prematurely white hair soon attracted the attention of influential state politicians. A contemporary described Clayton as "a tall, commanding, thoroughly well-developed figure, six feet one and a half inches high, with a handsome countenance molded in the style befitting great characters, and with an air of dignity, softened by that indefinable expression of the human face that shows a gentle heart in the breast." At the beginning of a long career of public service

John Middleton Clayton, distinguished lawyer, United States senator and secretary of state, assisted in the prosecution of Joe Johnson, which resulted in Johnson's conviction and flogging. *Courtesy of the Library of Congress.*

that included several terms as a United States senator and a stint as secretary of state, Clayton had been hired by Quakers to assist in the prosecution of Johnson, who was found guilty.

In early nineteenth-century Delaware, justice was swift and often brutal. When English colonists arrived in southern Delaware during the seventeenth century, they brought with them an attitude toward criminals that had its roots in the dark corners of the Middle Ages. After the colonists built a courthouse, they set up a whipping post and began flogging law-breakers into model citizens. When a colonist sang a "scurrilous, disgraceful song" that another settler found objectionable, the Sussex County court ordered that singer be fined "five hundred pounds of tobacco or whipped twenty-one lashes on the naked back."

It is not known whether the singer of the scurrilous, disgraceful song paid the fine or suffered the flogging, but such physical punishments were common in colonial Sussex County. Jails were temporary holding places for those awaiting trials. In place of incarceration, judges sentenced those found guilty of crimes to physical punishments that were immediate and brutal. Criminals were branded with hot irons, had their ears lopped off and, in the most severe cases, they were drawn and quartered. Many criminals paid for their crimes with a visit to the whipping post. In 1679, a Delaware woman was sentenced to twenty-one lashes after she bore three illegitimate children. When this sentence failed to convince her to change her ways, she was given another thirty-one lashes and banished from the colony. At the end of the

HARPER'S WEEKLY.

A JOURNAL OF CIVILIZATION

Vol. XII.—No. 624.] NEW YORK, SATURDAY, DECEMBER 12, 1868. [SINGLE COPIES, TEN CENTS. $4.00 PER YEAR IN ADVANCE.

Entered according to Act of Congress, in the Year 1868, by Harper & Brothers, in the Clerk's Office of the District Court of the United States, for the Southern District of New York.

THE WHIPPING-POST AND PILLORY AT NEW CASTLE, DELAWARE.—SKETCHED BY EARL SHINN.—[SEE PAGE 791.]

When Joe Johnson was flogged, the whipping post and the pillory in Georgetown were a simple post with the pillory attached to it, not the elaborated edifice at New Castle shown here in the December 12, 1868 issue of *Harper's Weekly. Courtesy of the Delaware Public Archives.*

American Revolution, a Delaware court found a group of Tories guilty of treason and sentenced them to the traditional punishment for treason: being drawn and quartered. Fortunately, the governor pardoned the Tories.

After the American Revolution, the county courthouse was moved to Georgetown, and a new whipping post and a set of stocks were built so that sentences could be carried out swiftly. Although most states abandoned corporal punishment of criminals, the whipping post remained an entrenched feature of the Delaware legal system.

Joe Johnson was convicted on one of the "bills of indictment found against him several years past, of kidnapping free Negroes" and sentenced to endure thirty-nine lashes, have his ears nailed to the pillory where he would remain for an hour and have the soft part of his ears cut off. A month after his conviction, several newspapers reported that on June 4, 1822, "The punishment upon Joseph Johnson was inflicted agreeable to the order of the Court, except the cutting off of the soft part of the ears, which was remitted by the Governor."

Did Her Good to See Him Beat the Boys

Joe Johnson's flogging was meant to deter him from kidnapping others, but it did not. The Baltimore abductions had taught Patty that ten or twelve victims could easily be abducted and confined aboard a small vessel, which could sail to the Nanticoke. From Cannon's Ferry, the captives could be marched to Johnson's Tavern or Patty's house for safekeeping until a vessel was available to take the victims to the South, where they could be sold with bogus bills of sale providing proof that the African Americans were slaves. With slaves fetching $300 apiece or more, a single drove could earn the gang a handsome $3,000 or $4,000. While Torrey was investigating the kidnappings in Delaware, Patty Cannon added to her crimes, abducting not just individuals but also mothers with infants and small children. On the slave market, these young children were not valuable. A buyer would have to invest several years raising the child before he or she would be able to perform productive labor. For Patty, these babies were a risk and an annoyance. When one of the babies was crying, she bashed his head in and killed him. On another occasion, one of the African American women gave birth to a light-skinned baby, and Patty believed that one of her relatives was the baby's father, so she killed the child. On another occasion, Cyrus James saw her attack a seven year old with a large stick. She beat him so badly that he died. The two infants and the seven-year-old were buried in a field near Patty's house.

After Johnson recovered from his wounds, Patty looked to the largest city in the United States, Philadelphia, for potential victims. Founded by the Quaker leader William Penn, Philadelphia was the home of the Declaration of Independence, the Constitution, the Liberty Bell and Quakers (the Society of Friends), whose beliefs in equality and pacifism led strident members to oppose the American Revolution and denounce slavery. In the early years, Quakers dominated the city government, but by the beginning of the nineteenth century, the burgeoning population of Philadelphia made members of the Society of Friends a minority. However, their beliefs continued to influence affairs in Philadelphia and Pennsylvania. Quakers were instrumental in founding the Society for the Relief of Free Negroes Unlawfully Held in Bondage, which became the Pennsylvania Abolition

In the early nineteenth century, Philadelphia was the largest city in the United States with an extensive waterfront along the Delaware River. The city had a large population of free persons of color who made tempting targets for Patty and her gang. *Courtesy of the Library of Congress.*

society, the first such group in the United States. In 1780, the abolitionists succeeded in passing a state law stating "that all persons...who shall be born within this state...shall not be deemed and considered as servants for life, or slaves; and that all servitude for life, or slavery of children, in consequence of the slavery of their mothers...shall be, and hereby is utterly taken away, extinguished and forever abolished."

Ten years after the passage of this law, there were only about three hundred slaves in Philadelphia, and the number of people held in perpetual bondage continued to decline as the African American population in the city continued to grow. Although they made up only about 10 percent of the total population, about eleven thousand people of color lived in Philadelphia at the time of the War of 1812. The large population of free people of color and the nearby slave states of Maryland and Delaware combined to make African Americans vulnerable to kidnapping and other schemes. At this time in Philadelphia, a man courted light-skinned females, married them and sold them as slaves. When this became known to Philadelphia's people of color, a mob formed and seized the kidnapping bigamist. According to the abolitionist writer Torrey, the heartless man was a "monster, in human shape" and he "was only saved from being torn in atoms, by being deposited in the city prison."

After Joe Johnson's flogging, Patty concluded that Philadelphia contained a large multitude of victims ripe for the picking. Patty and Joe Johnson planned to replicate the method used in Baltimore: use an accomplice to identify a target, entice the victim aboard a boat and set sail for the Nanticoke. Patty found a skilled and willing accomplice, a personable light-skinned man named John Purnell. A short man who could easily relate to younger victims sought by Patty's gang, Purnell often went by the name John Smith and other aliases. His playing a key role in the kidnapping operation, however, could prove to be a weak link in the chain that held Patty's band together.

Three years after Johnson's flogging, a number of free young people of color were reported missing in Philadelphia and its suburbs. At the time of their disappearance, some were believed to be victims of accidental drownings, and others were thought to be runaways from their parents, guardians or masters. In particular, several chimney sweeps were among the missing. The nature of their work took them out of their local neighborhoods, and very often, the chimney sweeps would not return home for several days, staying overnight at houses of friends or relatives. When some of the sweeps were apparently runaways who were reportedly seen in New York, Albany, Lancaster and other cities, there seemed to be no cause for undue alarm. In

1825, however, the number of missing chimney sweeps increased alarmingly during the summer. About twenty chimney sweeps had gone to work and not returned. Their friends and relatives concluded the worst, but they did not know that John Purnell was hard at work.

During the summer of 1825, Joe Johnson and Purnell set sail from the Nanticoke for Philadelphia. At that time, the Chesapeake and Delaware Canal would not open for another four years, and when the sloop reached the Chesapeake Bay, Johnson had to sail southward to the mouth of the bay and turn northward to cruise the length of the Delmarva Peninsula. Turning westward at the mouth of the Delaware Bay, Johnson and Purnell worked their way up the bay to Philadelphia, where they

Two nineteenth-century Philadelphia chimney sweeps photographed with the tools of their trade. *Courtesy of the Library of Congress.*

anchored in the middle of the Delaware River opposite the city's waterfront. After Johnson's sloop was anchored, Purnell used a small boat to go ashore.

The three blocks along the Delaware River waterfront north of Market Street were home to criminals, prostitutes, homeless, vagabonds and fugitive slaves, an area appropriately called "Hell Town." Purnell scanned anyone he passed for likely victims, and he carried a black sticking plaster that he pasted across the mouths of those he chose. Gagged by the plaster, they were unable to cry for help as Smith hustled them to Johnson's sloop. Purnell quickly bagged Enos Tilghman and Alexander Manlove and carried them to the sloop without difficulty. Once aboard the sailing vessel, Thomas Collins, one of Joe Johnson's henchmen, came down into the sloop's hold and said to kidnapped victims, "Now boys, be still. Make no noise, or I'll cut your throats."

Purnell returned ashore to look for additional victims when he encountered Samuel Scomp, a fifteen-year-old indentured servant who had run away from his master. Purnell offered to pay Scomp a quarter dollar to help bring a cargo of watermelons from the Navy Yard up to the Market Street wharf. Purnell and Scomp walked to the waterfront, where a boat came ashore from Johnson's sloop. As the boat with Purnell and his unsuspecting teenager was rowed toward the sloop, Purnell spotted Johnson standing on the deck, and Purnell called out, "Do you have watermelons to sell?" Johnson answered, "Plenty!" After the two black men climbed aboard the sloop, Johnson invited them into the cabin for a drink. Johnson lagged behind and left the teenager and Purnell alone in the cabin for a few minutes.

When Johnson, who towered over the teenage Scomp, entered the cabin, he was armed with a knife and threatened to cut Scomp's throat if he resisted or made a noise. Johnson directed the two black men to cross their hands so that he could tie them up with rope. Once Scomp and Purnell were bound, Johnson announced that Scomp and his father were slaves and that they had run away from their master in Maryland. After this astounding "revelation," Johnson turned to Purnell, who sat quietly while Johnson threatened Scomp, and untied him. Still maintaining the ruse, Johnson told Purnell to be off, saying, "Don't let me catch you here again." Purnell took the sloop's small boat and rowed ashore. After Purnell had left, Scomp was taken from the cabin and placed in the sloop's hold, where he found Tilghman and Manlove.

After Purnell returned to Philadelphia, he brought another victim, a short sixteen-year-old chimney sweep ironically named Joe Johnson, into the hold. An hour later, Purnell rowed out to the sloop with his last victim, Cornelius Sinclair. The hold of Johnson's sloop contained five young victims, who were entering their robust labor years and would sell for a premium price. In addition, the teenagers were going through rapid changes in their bodies that would make them more difficult to identify. According to one commentator at the time, "The absolute requirement of the verbal evidence of white persons in open court to identify the kidnapped person...[with] the lapse of a few years...[this] becomes almost impossible."

With their human cargo secured, Johnson raised anchor that night and sailed down the Delaware River to the mouth of the bay. Instead of traveling the length of the entire Delmarva Peninsula, after Johnson sailed around Cape Henlopen, he steered southward until he reached the Indian River Inlet where turned into the inlet and headed west. Entering the Indian River, Johnson anchored in the vicinity of Millsboro about two hours before sunset. The five captives, who had been in the dark hold for several days, were released from their leg irons and taken ashore. Ropes were strung around their necks, and they began to march through the marshes, cornfields and brushwood until they were put aboard a carriage driven by Johnson. Driven to Johnson's Tavern, the five kidnapped victims were taken to the garret and placed in irons. After a brief stay at Johnson's Tavern, the five were transferred to Jesse Cannon's house, where they were again placed in an attic and chained. After a week at Cannon's house, they were put into a wagon with two African American women: Mary Fisher, who was free and another kidnap victim, and Maria Neal, a slave. As Purnell drove the wagon, Ebenezer Johnson and his wife rode behind in a small, two-wheeled carriage. The African Americans were driven three miles to Patty Cannon's house.

After a brief stay at Patty's house, they were taken to the Nanticoke River, where they were put aboard a sloop and manacled in the hold. This vessel, larger than the one they were in on the Delaware, was big enough for an extended ocean voyage. In addition to the African Americans, on board were Ebenezer Johnson, his wife, Jesse Cannon and an old cook. The sloop sailed down the Nanticoke to the Chesapeake Bay and into the Atlantic. Cruising southward, the sloop was at sea for about a week when they landed in Alabama, where the kidnap victims began a grueling march northward across the state. The older and bigger prisoners were released of their chains while on the march. A one-horse wagon with some provisions and baggage was driven by the two smallest prisoners, Enos Tilghman and Alexander Manlove. The wagon was followed by Ebenezer and his wife in a gig. The prisoners were shoeless and marched about thirty miles each day. When they complained of sore feet and being unable to keep up the pace, the prisoners were flogged, and at one point, Scomp received more than fifty lashes at one time. Joe Johnson, the chimney sweep, and Cornelius Sinclair were the most frequently flogged. At Tuscaloosa, Sinclair was sold to a slave trader. As the remaining victims turned west toward Mississippi, the weather turned cold, and their feet started to freeze. Scomp had had enough. While on the march, the African Americans were unchained, and Scomp slipped away while in the areas controlled by the Choctaws, but he was caught by an Indian and returned to Johnson, who flogged Scomp with a hand saw and with hickory branches, raising deep cuts on his back and head that left permanent scars.

The party of prisoners remained for a month and a half near a small town called Ashville, within sixteen miles of the Cherokee nation. Johnson owned a log house and some land there. They then turned toward Rocky

Spring, Mississippi. The weather had turned cold, and the chimney sweep, Joe Johnson, fell frequently as he walked. After one severe beating with the cart whip, Ebenezer's wife remarked it did her good to see him beat the boys. Johnson, the chimney sweep, was so weak from the beatings and lame because of frozen feet that he was placed in the wagon, but the next day he died.

Finally, the march ended seven miles west of Rocky Springs, where Johnson sold all the kidnap victims, except for Maria Neal, to John W. Hamilton, a plantation owner. To verify his ownership of the African Americans, Johnson produced a fictitious bill of sale that was fabricated by Thomas Collins, a member of the gang, indicating that the kidnapped victims were slaves.

THE PHILADELPHIA CONNECTION

After Purnell delivered Scomp and the rest of the kidnap victims to Patty's house, he returned to the City of Brotherly Love to snare additional victims. In June 1825, Purnell decoyed another five victims, including at least one chimney sweep, aboard Joe Johnson's sloop that sailed down the Delaware past Cape Henlopen, where one of the captives got a glimpse of the lighthouse. After rounding the cape, Johnson followed the familiar route through the Indian River Inlet. After they landed, the five captives were chained together in a small oyster house for three days until they were loaded into a covered wagon and traveled overland, crossing the Nanticoke at Cannon's Ferry until they reached Johnson's Tavern. The five victims were taken to the garret, where they were chained to a large staple embedded in the floor.

Soon after the unfortunate five arrived, others began to be placed in the garret, including a cart driver, another two chimney sweeps and a young man who was abducted by Joe Johnson on the road in Sussex County. A total of twelve victims were chained to the same staple. In a separate room of the attic, two young women, Lydia Smith and Sally Nicholson, were also in chains. Lydia Smith, a native of southern Delaware, was supposed to receive her freedom when she turned twenty-one years of age, but she bounced around among several masters who kept her as an indentured servant until she was forcibly taken to Patty Cannon's house. Patty turned her over to Joe Johnson, and he passed her on to Jesse Cannon, who kept her in chains for five months. Lydia was taken back to Joe Johnson's Tavern and imprisoned in the attic. The prisoners were kept in the garret about six months until one night the twelve men and two women were taken from the attic and marched to the Nanticoke River.

Once Johnson's fourteen captives reached the Nanticoke, he put them on board a ship and set sail. About six days later, they landed near Baltimore. Like the group that Ebenezer Johnson took to Mississippi, Joe Johnson chained the larger men two and two. He allowed the younger captives to travel unfettered. Although a group of African Americans chained together on the roads of Maryland and Virginia was a common sight, Johnson, perhaps smarting from his flogging, wanted to avoid any unnecessary encounters, and he used back roads and camped out where convenient. Joe Johnson strictly ordered the captives not to talk to anyone that they happened to meet, but some ignored the order, and that led to serious consequences. If Joe found out that any of his prisoners had said that they were free, he severely flogged them. Finally, the captives reached Rockingham, North Carolina, where Joe Johnson sold all of the African Americans, who were split up and sold to various masters. Some fetched as much as $450.

While business seemed to be good for Patty and her gang, they had made a serious mistake. Thinking that the abducted blacks were far away from help, they did not count on the determination of several white people in Pennsylvania and Mississippi to get to the source of these kidnappings. As John Hamilton looked at the African Americans, he sensed that something was wrong. Hamilton questioned Ebenezer Johnson, who claimed that the blacks were all legal and offered as support the bogus bill of sale that had been fabricated by Thomas Collins, one of the gang's henchmen. Hamilton was unconvinced. He may have heard snatches of conversation from the supposed slaves that they were free. A justice of the peace was called and threatened to arrest Johnson, but Ebenezer said that he had further proof that the African Americans were slaves. In good faith, he agreed to let the blacks remain at Hamilton's plantation, and Johnson left to retrieve the documents that would show that his captives were slaves.

With Ebenezer Johnson gone, Samuel Scomp told the details of his kidnapping to Hamilton, who was convinced that he was telling the truth. Hamilton called his lawyer, John Henderson, and the two drafted a detailed letter to Joseph Watson, the mayor of Philadelphia. Born in 1764, Watson was a carpenter and lumber merchant who was first elected as an alderman in 1822. Two years later, the city council elected him to be mayor, a post that he held for four years. In November 1824, he learned of the case of Isaiah Sadler, who had been kidnapped in Philadelphia and sold into slavery.

Placed in irons, Sadler splintered the handle of a wooden spoon to pick the lock and escape, but the poor treatment had left him a cripple.

When Watson received Hamilton and Henderson's letter, he turned it over to the newspapers, and this caught the attention of James Rogers, the attorney general of Delaware. Rogers, who knew that Joe Johnson had been flogged for kidnapping in 1822, had been following the activities of the Johnson brothers for years. Immediately Rogers wrote to Watson, "Joseph is perhaps the most celebrated kidnapper and Negro stealer in the country, and perhaps no case can occur where such efficient means should be used to bring both these persons particularly Joseph to the bar of justice."

Rogers believed that only through prompt action and proper evidence could one of the ringleaders of Patty's gang be arrested, but Joseph eluded capture despite several "unsuccessful efforts [that] were made for about 3 to 5 years before he was arrested in this state on a charge of kidnapping." There seemed to be a mistaken belief that the Johnsons lived in Virginia, but, as Rogers pointed out, "their place of residence is not in Virginia but within a few feet of the line dividing this state from Maryland near Nanticoke River and distant from Laurel in the county of Sussex of this state about 9 miles or perhaps some little more."

Unfortunately, the members of the Cannon-Johnson gang operated freely, because, as Rogers said, "little reliance can be placed for their arrest by persons in their immediate neighborhood." The Delaware attorney general, however, stated that he would cooperate with the Pennsylvania authorities: "Should [they] intend to make an attempt to punish these persons I will cheerfully afford any advice or information in my power to give to facilitate such object."

In addition, Rogers received a letter from Georgetown resident Thomas S. Layton, who also read Watson's letters and had done some investigating about John Smith and Thomas Collins. He could not find anything about Collins, but there was a light-skinned man who went by the name of Spencer Francis who Layton strongly suspected of being John Purnell. According to Layton, Purnell was seen the previous summer in company with Johnson and "was leaping to and from Philadelphia often in the summer and fall." In addition, "a black man belonging to Mrs. T.J.C. Wright of Cannon's Ferry, who made his escape last summer, has been taken and says that Spencer [Purnell] passed under the name of John Smith in Philadelphia."

Rogers was determined to break the back of the Cannon gang, and he wrote to Watson, "If either or both of them should take up a situation within this state I shall direct their arrest." But this would not be a simple matter, and Rogers needed the full effort by the Pennsylvania authorities. As he stated, "To accomplish the arrest of these men will require more than ordinary perseverance from the public authority of your state."

The resourceful mayor of Philadelphia also assigned Samuel Garrigues, whom Watson considered "one of the high constables of this city[,] an excellent officer and fully possessing my confidence," to investigate the kidnappings. To satisfy the requirement that a white person testify as to the identity of the abducted free blacks, Watson found a resident of Philadelphia who was willing to travel to Alabama to indentify Cornelius Sinclair and have him returned to his home.

All of these efforts would be useless, however, unless the authorities in the South cooperated. Watson got in touch with Richard Stockton, the attorney general for Mississippi, who lent the full weight of his office to help free the kidnap victims. Furthermore, Stockton suggested sending the victims back to their homes while the legal process worked out. In addition, he wrote, "It is the subject of deep regret to me that proper measures were not taken to ascertain the cause of the death of one of the unfortunate youths, at the time the rest were stopped. There is no doubt upon my mind, but that he was cruelly and barbarously murdered."

When Garrigues arrived to help transport the kidnap victims back to their homes, Mary Fisher was afraid to return to Pennsylvania by sea. She decided to wait on Hamilton's plantation, where she was treated as a free person, until she could travel by land. Despite Mississippi being a slave state, Stockton contended, "There is no community that holds in greater abhorrence, the infamous traffic carried on by Negro stealers." He maintained that a simple petition to the Circuit Court would enable the victims to be released, and he claimed, "Public feeling is uniformly enlisted in favor of the petitioning slave, the bar are ever ready to tender their professional services."

Stockton wrote, "Good slaves may be stolen or seduced from good masters; husbands, wives and children may be separated from each other, it is true, by the cunning and management of the kidnapper," but the fear of free people of color remained strong: "[As] much [as] we might be disposed to liberate a free Negro from the irons of the wretch who stole him, yet for the most part free negroes are the worst description of people that could even willingly be brought among us."

As Garrigues was retrieving Patty's kidnap victims in Mississippi, Watson was determined to destroy her gang. He said, "The mazes of this infernal plot, by which a great number of free born children, during several years past, have been seduced away…by a gang of desperadoes, whose haunts and headquarters are known to have been, on the dividing line between the states of Delaware and Maryland, low down on the peninsula, between the Delaware and Chesapeake bays."

In an effort to gain additional information about the Cannon-Johnson gang, on February 9, 1827, Watson issued a proclamation that stated:

> *Whereas, information has been received, that in the year 1825, a number of free persons of color, principally children, inhabitants of the city and county of Philadelphia, were forcibly seized by persons then unknown and carried into slavery…I, Joseph Watson, Mayor of said city, do hereby offer a reward of Five Hundred Dollars for the apprehension and prosecution to conviction of any person concerned in the forcible abduction of the free colored persons from the city of Philadelphia.*

A Career of Iniquity

As Mayor Watson waited to see if the reward offer would produce enough evidence to arrest Patty, detective Garrigues returned from Tuscaloosa, Alabama, where the tenacious constable had rescued Cornelius Sinclair. All of those who had been purchased by the Mississippi plantation owner John Hamilton were also back in Philadelphia or were in good hands. To thank Hamilton and his lawyer, John Henderson, Mayor Watson arranged to have two silver pitchers valued at $150 each sent to these men with the inscription, "In commemoration of the disinterested, spirited and benevolent exertions of [John Henderson on one and J.W. Hamilton on the other] of Mississippi, in rescuing from the unlawful bondage, certain persons of color, who had by force or fraud been taken from their homes in the states of Pennsylvania and Maryland, this piece of plate is respectfully presented by a number of citizens of Philadelphia. March, 1827."

With Garrigues back in Philadelphia, Watson considered how best to employ this dogged detective to disrupt the kidnappers. Joe Johnson was a convicted kidnapper, and Patty Cannon had long been suspected of being involved with the abductions, but the authorities struggled to get concrete evidence against her. The location of her house enabled her to hide behind a cloud of confused jurisdictions, but if the mayor of Philadelphia, the attorney general of Delaware and the local authorities all cooperated, the legal obstructions could be overcome. In the meantime, Mayor Watson decided to focus on the weak link in Patty's gang: John Purnell.

As the decoy who enticed many kidnap victims aboard Joe Johnson's sloop, Purnell knew the inner workings of the gang. If he could be captured and made to talk, as had happened with Jesse Griffith, Patty could, at last, be brought to justice. The problem was that Purnell cloaked his nefarious activities behind several aliases and was known to be a resourceful character. Watson, however, assigned Garrigues, who was equally resourceful, to find and apprehend Purnell.

After Garrigues was put on the case and began to make inquires, Purnell learned that someone was asking questions about him, and the kidnapper quickly left southern Delaware. Taking a sailing ship, Purnell landed in Boston, where there was a significant population of free people of color. With his engaging personality and his gift for creating aliases, Purnell might easily have blended in. The fugitive, however, did not cover his tracks well. Garrigues learned of Purnell's escape to Boston, and the detective sent to the authorities in Massachusetts incriminating information about the sly kidnapper. Having done this, Garrigues was soon on a ship beating its way northward to the Massachusetts town.

Purnell could not have hoped to find refuge in the white population of Boston, and when the black population learned of his crimes, they were equally loath to protect him. Boston residents were happy to identify the newly arrived stranger. It only took a short time for the Boston authorities to tract down and arrest Purnell, and when Garrigues arrived in town, they turned the kidnapper over to the Philadelphia constable. Garrigues was quickly headed back to Philadelphia with Purnell in tow.

Arriving back in Philadelphia, Purnell was charged with two counts of kidnaping. At that time, the Pennsylvania criminal justice system was far different from that of Delaware or Maryland. When William Penn founded the colony, Quakers, who had been persecuted for their religion and had felt the wrath of the courts in England and America, had a different perspective on crime and punishment. In Pennsylvania, criminals were more likely to be fined and incarcerated rather than flogged and publicly humiliated. In addition, Pennsylvania courts allowed the testimony of African Americans, and several of Purnell's victims were brought to Philadelphia to confront their kidnapper.

Cornelius Sinclair, who was sold in Tuscaloosa and rescued by Garrigues, identified Purnell as the man who had used the alias "John Smith" and the one who had lured him aboard the sloop in Philadelphia. Sinclair also testified that Purnell used a black sticking plaster to gag two of the victims to prevent them from calling out when they were abducted. According to the

African Observer, "One of them, a boy about ten years of age, thus gagged, appears to have been carried off in open day, and the other in the dusk of the evening."

Another one of Purnell's victims, Samuel Scomp, testified that he had been lured aboard the sloop to help unload watermelons, which, Scomp said, was "a marvelously good joke at being decoyed in this manner." The African American's stereotypical comment brought a round of laughter in the courtroom.

Purnell was found guilty on two counts of kidnapping and sentenced to pay a fine of $4,000 and be imprisoned for forty-two years. The *African Observer* commented, "By the indefatigable exertions of the mayor of this city [Philadelphia], aided by the personal exertions of S.P. Garrigues, high constable, this man has at length been stopped in his career of iniquity...It is to be hoped, that by the year 1869 [when Purnell was due to be released], the trade of stealing children will be rendered unprofitable."

The *Niles Register* reported wryly, "This fellow's kidnapping days are over."

The apprehension and conviction of Purnell cost Patty one of her strongest henchmen, but the investigation of Purnell may have alerted Patty and the Johnson brothers that the authorities were getting closer. If the inquiries about Purnell's actions had been handled more discreetly, evidence may have been developed that directly implicated Patty and Joe and Ebenezer Johnson. Joe Johnson and his brother, apparently not wishing to wait around to find out if the authorities had enough evidence to charge them, fled Delaware. Unlike Jesse Griffith, Purnell did not implicate other gang members when he was arrested. Two years after Purnell's conviction, Cyrus James and a henchman named Butler were arrested on suspicion of kidnapping, but Patty did not seem to be worried. She was then over sixty years old and a widow. There were rumors that she had poisoned her husband, Jesse, but that has never been substantiated. She appeared to be content to retire to her rocking chair, secure in the belief that the lack of evidence and her feminine charms could ward off any attempt by the authorities to arrest her.

Seduced by the Devil

The conviction of John Purnell was not the only change for Patty and her gang. By 1829, occasional steamboats puffing clouds of dark smoke came chugging up the Nanticoke River. The steamboats were able to travel to Baltimore,

Washington and other Chesapeake ports without regard to wind and weather. Work had also begun on the northern part of the Delmarva Peninsula on a canal that would link Delaware and Chesapeake Bays. The canal would one day make travel from the Nanticoke River to Philadelphia easier, but if Patty entertained thoughts of reopening the Philadelphia connection for kidnapped people of color, she was wrong. She was not the robust woman that she had once been. It is doubtful that she could wrestle a kidnap victim into submission, and her youthful charms had faded, but she appeared to be content to live out the remaining years of her life in peace. Thieves, kidnappers and other criminals are not known for their financial planning, but the cash from scores of kidnapped victims who were sold into slavery and the money robbed from the slave traders would have provided Patty with a considerable sum for her golden years. In addition, she was able to rent land surrounding her home to a farmer, and that would have generated a modest income. Her life of crime seemed to have paid off handsomely.

In April 1829, winter had ended, and the trees were beginning to bud. It was time for spring planting, and Patty's tenant farmer was plowing a field near her house. He decided to tackle a low-lying spot that had been covered with brush for many years. Once the bushes and weeds were cut and cleared, the farmer stepped behind the plow and signaled the horse to move ahead. As the horse trod into the dip in the field, the farmer was startled to see the animal sink into the ground up to its haunches. The farmer extricated his horse from the ground and dug through the dirt to see why the ground was so soft. Within minutes after digging through the loose soil, he uncovered a three-foot long blue chest. Quickly, he opened the chest and discovered it was filled with human bones. Here, at last, was evidence that the stories about Patty Cannon robbing and murdering were true!

The tenant farmer abandoned his plowing for the day and rushed to tell others what he had found. The news spread quickly, as neighbors across central Delmarva rushed to tell one another that bones had been found in the field near Patty's house. Soon, people from miles around were flocking to the field to see for themselves the blue chest full of bones. Some recalled that ten or twelve years ago, a slave trader from Georgia with $15,000 in his pocket to buy slaves had failed to return home. Some said the trader's name was Bell, others said it was Miller and still others said it was Bell Miller or Miller Bell. The important fact was that Patty was later found to have his horse, which she claimed he had left when he returned to Georgia with a cargo of African Americans. The crowd agreed that the bones in the blue chest must be those of the missing slave trader.

The excitement at Patty Cannon's house increased when the authorities brought Cyrus James and Butler from Georgetown, where they were being held on suspicion of kidnapping. James, raised by Patty from the age of seven, had participated in a number of her misdeeds and witnessed many more. Up until this point, he had been loyal to her, but with Jesse Cannon, Patty's husband, and the Johnson brothers gone, things were changing. When James was shown the bone-filled box, he declared that Joseph Johnson, Ebenezer F. Johnson and old Patty Cannon had shot the man while at supper in her house and he saw them all engaged in carrying him in the chest and burying him.

With that admission out of the bag, James said that many others had been murdered, and he could literally show where the bodies were buried. James led the authorities—and an eager crowd following their every step—into the field next to the Cannon house. He pointed out the burial places as best he could remember them, and the crowd attacked the site with shovels like wild hogs rooting for food. In one place, a garden, they dug and found the bones of a young child whose mother, James said, was a black woman belonging to Patty. When the baby was born with light skin, Patty suspected the father to be one of her own family, and she had killed the child.

When James pointed out another place a few feet away, the crowd immediately began to dig. When they dug a hole a few feet deep, they uncovered two oak boxes containing human bones. In one box, the bones appeared to be of a person about seven years of age. James recounted how he had seen Patty knock the youngster in the head with a billet of wood. The other was a child whom Patty considered "bad property," which, at the time of the discovery was thought to have meant that the child was free, but it probably meant that the child was too young to be sold for a good profit.

James said that often the captured children would not keep quiet, and there was no convenient opportunity to send them away, so they were murdered to prevent discovery. On examining the skull bone of the largest child, it was discovered to have been broken as described by James. Years after the discovery of the rudimentary graves in Patty's yard, a story arose about a particularly heartless murder. One of Patty's captive women had a little child about five years old who was restless and screamed constantly. Patty became so annoyed that she picked up the child and beat him. Despite Patty's pummeling, the child continued to scream. She tore his clothes off, held the screaming child's face to the blazing fire in the fireplace and scorched him to death. The story of this incident, which Cyrus James did not mention as the bones were uncovered, first appeared over a decade after Patty's death and has not been substantiated by other contemporary sources.

The discovery of the bones by the Cannon house and the testimony of Cyrus James provided enough tangible evidence to link Patty Cannon with some of the murders that she had been rumored to have committed through the years. With Joe Johnson, rumored to be in Alabama, and her other principal henchmen gone, Patty had to rely on her charm to avoid arrest. For once, her feminine allure failed her, and she was taken into custody immediately. According to the *Delaware Gazette*, "This woman is now between 60 and 70 years of age, and looks more like a man than a woman; but old as she is, she is believed to be heedless and heartless as the most abandoned wretch that breathes."

Convinced that they now had enough evidence to convict Patty, she was taken, along with James and Butler, to Georgetown and lodged in the jail in the center of town. At Patty's house, a small mob of people continued to plow up the turf looking for additional graves, According to the *Delaware Gazette*, "James stated that he had not shown all the places where murdered bodies had been buried, and at the time of writing, our correspondent informs us the people were still digging." The newspaper also speculated about a future trial that

> *will present the wretched actors in the scenes of blood, which have taken place on the border of our state in Sussex county...The neighborhood in which these terrible events occurred, the borders of Delaware and Maryland, has long been famous for negro stealing and negro trading— and "Patty Cannon" and "Joe Johnson" are familiar names to us. The people thereabouts were exceeding ignorant and desperately wicked—but we hope that some improvement has latterly taken place.*

The report in the *Delaware Gazette* was printed in other newspapers, including the *Niles Weekly Register*, a highly regarded Baltimore newspaper with a wide readership. On April 25, the *Niles Weekly Register* printed the *Gazette* account under the headline "A HORRIBLE DEVELOPMENT...The murders in Sussex."

On April 13, 1829, at the old courthouse in Georgetown, Attorney General Rogers indicted Patty on three of the most heinous, and perhaps the most provable, crimes that she had committed. With great formality and laced with nineteenth-century legalese, the indictment alleged that Patty had cold-bloodedly murdered three infants on April 26, 1822. According to the indictment:

Patty Cannon late of North West Fork Hundred, in the County aforesaid, widow, not having the fear of God before her eyes, but being moved and seduced by the instigation of the Devil...[took a] certain infant female child...lately born and being alive in the Peace of God and of the State of Delaware then and there being feloniously, willfully and of her malice aforethought did make an assault, and that the said Patty Cannon, with both her hands about the neck of the said infant female child...did choke and strangle, of which said choking and strangling the said infant female child...then and there instantly died.

Having killed one infant, Patty moved on to a second baby. The indictment alleged, "The said Patty Cannon...[did] throw the said infant female child... being alive upon the ground, and...[did] cover over with earth...suffocated [her]...[and the infant] instantly died." With two female babies dead, Patty turned to the third infant. According to the indictment, she took the male infant "into both her hands and...fixed about the neck...did choke and strangle...said infant male child...[and he] instantly died."

Using the headline "MURDERS IN DELAWARE," the *Niles Register* reported the charges against Patty and stated that the grand jury had also indicted Joe Johnson and Ebenezer Johnson. The newspaper noted that the Johnson brothers "reside out of state—where, is not exactly known, but we take it for granted, that the proper steps will be to discover and bring them to justice."

It appeared that Georgetown would host a sensational trial at the old wooden courthouse followed by an execution that would surely attract more spectators than the hangings of Griffith and Brereton in 1813, but that did not happen. In a hastily added postscript to the article that described the plans for the trial, the *Niles Register* reported, "Patty Cannon died in jail on the 11th instant."

Chapter 3
The Historical Legacy of Patty Cannon

THE TRADE IS LIKELY TO THRIVE

Patty Cannon was found dead in her cell; the cause of her death unknown. Sixty or seventy years old, she may not have been able to bear the trauma of her arrest and impending trial, but eight years after her death, Senator John M. Clayton, who had assisted in the 1822 kidnapping trial of Joe Johnson, wrote, "This demon took arsenic and died by her own hand." With Patty's death and the Johnson brothers gone for parts unknown, the volume of kidnapping of free people of color declined. Michael Millman moved into Patty's old house where, according to Clayton, "so many murders were committed on the kidnapped Negroes and others who had been inmates of or visitors to the mansion." Millman found the building equipped with shackles, perfect for confining kidnapped victims and others. In 1837, Senator Clayton wrote:

[The house] *is in Dorchester County Maryland and within a stone's cast of Caroline County in Maryland and Sussex County in Delaware. It has been the old stand and residence of the most celebrated kidnappers and murderers this county has produced. Johnson himself made fortune at the business and easily escaped justice by removing from one county or state to another when pursued by an officer with posse, for none but an officer with a posse could take him.*

Senator Clayton also reported that two Sussex County residents, Houston and Wilson, were searching for kidnapped African Americans when they entered the house and discovered several people of color in chains. The two men could not ascertain whether most of the captives were slave or free, but one of the men recognized an apprentice who was chained along with the others. John Whaley, the master of the apprentice, had given him over to Millman to sell along with the others. According to Clayton, "Among the Negroes in chains, there [was] the poor apprentice boy of John Whaley. Houston knew him and despite of threats and dangers brought him off after he had knocked off his chains."

Whaley was arrested and convicted of kidnapping, but he was given a pardon, which infuriated Clayton, who wrote, "It was decidedly the most outrageous case of kidnapping I ever heard tried and was proved as conclusively by a dozen or twenty witnesses." The case was so clear that Whaley's attorneys "did not attempt to argue the fact to the jury, who convicted the prisoner on the whole indictment almost immediately." According to Clayton, "There was not a single redeeming circumstance in the whole case—the prisoner did not dare to put his reputation in issue for his was an old offender against the law." Clayton went on to comment, "As he is pardoned...and as the other kidnappers have all escaped, the trade is like[ly] to thrive."

Kidnapping in Sussex continued, in part, because attitudes of the people of central Delmarva had changed little in the decades when Paul Cuffee docked in Vienna with a crew of free people of color and caused a minor panic. In 1831, Nat Turner, a slave from Southampton, Virginia, armed with a hatchet entered his master's bedroom and hacked him to death, igniting a bloody slave revolt. By the time that Turner and his followers were finished, over fifty people had been killed, and the fear of a slave rebellion spread quickly throughout the South.

Turner's bloody rampage sent shivers down the spines of residents of Maryland, Delaware and other slave states. In the area near the Nanticoke River, rumors spread that bands of runaway slaves were gathering in the Great Cypress Swamp, and a band of hooligans decided to play a prank. On Election Day in 1831, when there were already rumors of an impending black uprising, the pranksters assembled on the banks of the Nanticoke River within sight of the town of Seaford. They divided into two groups, one of which brandished firearms. The group with the guns lagged behind the others, who started running toward the town. The other pranksters pretended to fire on the others, some of whom fell to the ground pretending to be shot, and others ran into Seaford spreading the news that a band of African Americans had landed a short distance from Seaford and had killed several white men. The marauding band of blacks, the pranksters said, were marching on Seaford bent on causing havoc and destruction.

The practical joke fed the latent fears of the white population of Delmarva and created a panic. Some residents fled to the forest to hide until the marauders passed. Others took up arms to confront the supposed band of desperados in deadly combat. The news of the alleged uprising, now estimated at 1,500 armed African Americans marching along the banks of the Nanticoke, spread across Delaware. Many communities attempted to disarm all people of color, free or slave, and towns prepared for war as if to meet an army of foreign invaders.

Unlike Patty's real kidnapping of scores of African Americans that caused barely a ripple on Delmarva, the practical joke resulted in the passage of a series of repressive laws aimed at curbing the activities of free blacks. These laws made it illegal for free African Americans to own firearms or hold religious meetings. Many whites believed that the black churches were fomenting rebellion, and so religious services could only be held under the supervision of "respectable white persons." In addition, out-of-state African American preachers, who were suspected of bringing plans of insurrection to Delaware, were banned. Violators were subject to be sold as slaves.

The African American residents of Sussex County had a few years to adjust to these Draconian laws when William Yates, an agent for the American Anti-Slavery Society, arrived in Delaware to observe conditions of people of color. Yates found that the laws passed after Nat Turner's Rebellion were designed to reduce the power and influence of people of color. In addition, the Delaware law that made it illegal to sell slaves to out-of-state buyers was being ignored. These added restrictions on people of color put African Americans further away from the normal protections of the law and made it easier (as Senator Clayton said) for kidnappers to thrive.

Money Was His God

Patty was not the only member of the Cannon family who caused hardship and pain to the residents of central Delmarva. When James Cannon established a ferry across the Nanticoke River, he had no idea that he was launching one of the most cold-hearted banking enterprises ever to exist in southern Delaware. At the time of the American Revolution, the lack of a steady supply of currency remained a serious problem, and the break from England only made matters worse. In 1785, a storm drove the *Faithful Steward*, laden with a cargo of English copper coins, onto the Delaware shore and scattered the vessel's cargo of coins along the coast. Remnants of the *Faithful Steward*'s cargo are still found north of Indian River Inlet in an area known as "coin beach."

In the nineteenth century, the shortage of currency led to an informal banking system in which those who had accumulated money would lend it to their neighbors. The free African American Levin Thompson treated those who borrowed money from him with respect, but when Isaac and Jacob Cannon engaged in similar activities, they were far less compassionate. Isaac and Jacob were second cousins once removed of Jesse Cannon, Patty's husband, and shared her penchant for greed and cruelty.

When James Cannon (who operated the ferry in the eighteenth century) died, he left his land, two houses and the ferry to his son Isaac with the provision that his widow, Betty, be allowed to live in one of the houses. Betty, Isaac and Jacob, Isaac's younger brother, operated the ferry for over a half century, and they tried to squeeze every penny out of the operation. Travelers were required to assist in rowing the ferry scow across the river, and because the boat was so small, they had to make multiple trips, one for their carriage and another for their horses. In addition, there was no inn on either side of the river, and travelers grumbled that there was no place to eat or sleep until they reached Johnson's Tavern or Laurel. There were also complaints that the ferry scow was left unattended, and travelers had to wait in the rain and snow for hours before someone would come to help row the people across.

Despite their neglect, Betty, Isaac and Jacob earned a steady income from the ferry. Charging five cents for each person and horse, ten cents for every two-wheeled carriage and thirty cents for every four-wheeled carriage, the Cannon brothers parlayed the steady income from the ferry into a variety of ventures. Isaac and Jacob improved the road that led to the ferry, acquired several thousand acres of Sussex County land and operated several vessels that sailed out of Seaford. The Cannon family also owned over two dozen slaves, which placed them among the largest slave-holding families in southern Delaware. Around 1820, Jacob Cannon built a stately two-story frame mansion that faced the Nanticoke near the ferry landing. The building had a fine view of the river and was dubbed Cannon Hall, which Jacob, it is said, intended to share with his bride-to-be. Unfortunately, Jacob's fiancée either died or jilted him at the last minute, and he never lived in the building.

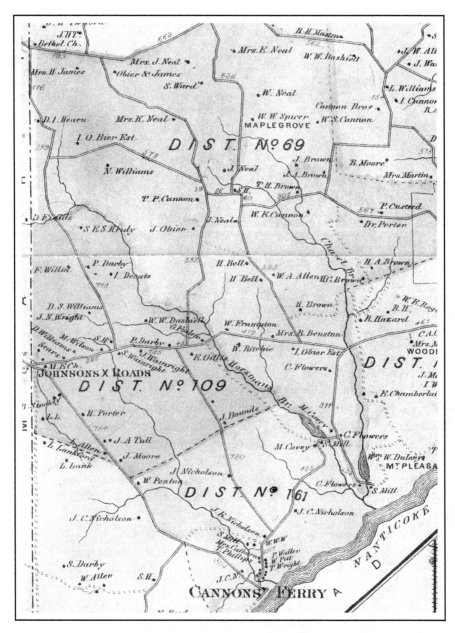

On this mid-nineteenth century map, Cannon's Ferry is at the bottom center, and Johnson's Crossroads is on the left edge near the center. Patty's house would have been a little north of Johnson's Crossroads near the left edge of the map. *Courtesy of the Delaware Public Archives.*

Cannon Hall, one of the largest houses in western Sussex County, overlooks the Nanticoke River, several hundred yards from the ferry landing. *Courtesy of the Delaware Public Archives.*

The Cannon brothers lent some of their excess capital to their Sussex County neighbors. At a time when banking was totally unregulated, the Cannon brothers became infamous for charging exorbitant interest rates and quickly confiscating goods that had been put up as collateral. Unlike their notorious relative Patty, the two brothers always remained within the letter of the law. Nonetheless, they were said to have confiscated dinner pots with hot food in them and to have taken the beds from under the dying to satisfy a sheriff's sale. The hard-hearted attitude of the Cannon brothers was well known, especially by those who worked for them.

In 1818, the Cannon brothers acquired the schooner *Baraco*, and they hired Nathaniel Raymond to captain the boat, which they used in the coastal trade. After stopping in Baltimore in November 1820, Raymond and a crew of five men set sail for Santo Domingo. Among the crewmen was the slave George Rayner. Some slaves were expert seamen, but Rayner's position on the *Baraco* is not known. He may have been a sailor, or he could have been the schooner's cook. In either case, when the *Baraco* reached Cape Haiti, Santo Domingo, Rayner fled the schooner.

In an affidavit filed later, Captain Raymond stated, "Every possible exertion was made by the Master and officers to get him back, and a reward of twenty dollars was offered for his apprehension. On the ninth day of January 1821, the said George Rayner was taken up and lodge in the Guardhouse for safe keeping; but on the tenth following, the Master went ashore in the boat for him, he found that he had been suffered to escape."

Around noon on the same day, Rayner was recaptured and taken to the town jail. He escaped again. Captain Raymond went ashore again and recaptured Rayner a second time. This time, Raymond decided not to leave the fugitive slave in the porous Cape Haiti jail. Raymond took Rayner aboard the *Baraco*, where he could be guarded closely.

The next morning, a small boat with a government official and several armed men rowed out to the *Baraco* and demanded the release of Rayner. There was little that Raymond could do, and Rayner was taken ashore. During the next several days, Raymond made several protests to the local government officials, but they steadfastly refused to release the fugitive slave. Reluctantly, Captain Raymond raised anchor and set sail for America, where he prepared for the wrath of Jacob and Isaac Cannon when they would learn that their slave had escaped in Santo Domingo.

The ire of the Cannon brothers, whether directed at those who worked for them or their creditors, earned them many enemies. William Morgan, a nineteenth-century resident of lower Delaware, kept a journal of happenings in southern Sussex County, and most of his comments were sober and unemotional. Morgan, a medical doctor and a Methodist preacher, had an intense dislike for the Cannon brothers, as did Owen O'Day, who was said to be a former member of Patty's gang. On April 12, 1842, Jacob Cannon, wearing two heavy coats, stepped off the ferry, when he encountered Owen O'Day, who had been the victim of Cannon's heavy-handed loan practices. Jacob had accused O'Day of stealing a bee gum, the section of tree that contained a beehive. When O'Day found that there was no legal remedy to use against Cannon, he loaded his musket and went looking for the loan shark. When O'Day saw Jacob leaving the ferryboat, he opened fire. O'Day's shot peppered Jacob's chest and arm, but his thick clothing prevented the pellets from hitting any vital organs. Seeing Cannon staggered by the blast from his musket, O'Day pulled out a pistol and fired again at the unscrupulous moneylender. The pistol shot seemed to have little effect on Cannon, who was now bleeding profusely from the many small wounds caused by the musket blast.

Cannon was able to stumble home, and doctors were summoned to treat him. After they peeled the blood-soaked coat and shirts from Cannon's body, the doctors discovered twenty holes in Jacob's clothing. According to Morgan, they found no indication "that any shot had entered his vitals." The doctors decided Cannon needed rest to help him recover from his wounds, and they gave him a heavy dose of the opiate laudanum, which in the nineteenth century was prescribed for a wide variety of ailments ranging from simple aches and pains to heart disease. Morgan, who was also a medical doctor, noted, "It appears the doctors gave him at least a hundred and twenty drops of strong laudanum, to put him to sleep, which it did to a certainty, for he never awoke."

After Cannon had died, a coroner's inquest determined that pellets fired by O'Day had penetrated Cannon's left lung and that the loan shark had died from the shotgun blast. Despite this evidence, it was popularly held that the laudanum administered by the doctors killed Jacob Cannon. So hated was Jacob Cannon that even though Owen O'Day was widely known to have killed him, after O'Day was indicted for murder, the people of central Delmarva allowed him to escape arrest.

Jacob Cannon was buried in the small cemetery near Cannon Hall overlooking the river. A month after Jacob's murder, Isaac became sick, and the doctors could do nothing for him. As his strength ebbed, Isaac calculated the principal and interest that he was still owed and had his money counted,

A small cemetery on the western bank of the Nanticoke River at Cannon's Ferry houses the graves of Jacob Cannon (left) and his brother Isaac (right). *Photo by Michael Morgan.*

wrapped and labeled. The dying man briefly turned from his accounts to scold his servants. With only a few minutes of life left, Cannon "cursed and raved like a devil, at some supposed neglect or inaccuracy in planting his garden." On May 6, Morgan reported: "Today the great and rich Isaac Cannon of Cannon's Ferry died about 10 o'clock a.m. Well, the mighty man is dead." Morgan then gave his final assessment of Isaac and Jacob: "After fifty years, cheating, oppressing, and distressing, selling and taking every thing they could lay hold of there they lie in graves unlamented and unmourned by any except a few flatterers. One of his oppression and cruelty was shot in cold blood and died as a beast. The other was permitted to die in his bed! But money was his God."

Follow the Drinking Gourd

It would be unfair to say that Harriet Tubman was a neighbor to Patty Cannon. Tubman was born a slave around 1820, though the evidence conflicts on the exact date, which would make her about nine years old when Patty died. Tubman lived the early part of her life about twenty-five miles from Cannon's house, working as a field hand and house servant on a farm between the Nanticoke and Choptank Rivers in Maryland. Although Harriet and Patty were not neighbors, it would not be unreasonable to conclude that Tubman was aware of the kidnapping gang and the dangers of traveling along the Nanticoke into Delaware.

Although Tubman may not have known the details of Patty's kidnapping exploits, Harriet personally experienced the agony of having family members ruthlessly separated. Coming from a large family, many of Tubman's brothers and sisters had been sold to plantation owners in the South. In 1844, she married John Tubman, a free black. Five years later, Harriet learned that she was about to be sold, and she resolved to escape. After Nat Turner's bloody rebellion in 1831, slave states passed laws that made it illegal to teach slaves to read and write. Unable to read signposts, runaway slaves had to rely on directions from strangers, who often betrayed runaway slaves to collect rewards offered by the fugitives' masters. Despite the risk, Tubman, who was illiterate, decided that she would have gain her freedom or die trying, and in 1849, she slipped away from her master's plantation and headed north.

When she began her flight for freedom, Tubman followed the Choptank River, which flowed out of central Delaware southward

Depicted in *Still's Underground Railroad Records*, a large group of twenty-eight fugitives, some from Cambridge, Maryland, make their way across the Delmarva Peninsula to Pennsylvania and freedom. *Courtesy of the Library of Congress.*

through Maryland. Walking by night and hiding by day, not knowing whom to trust or how close her pursuers might be, she carefully felt her way northward. Using her natural cunning, Tubman successfully avoided the slave-catchers and was able to find houses where friendly people gave her food and sometimes shelter. She often slept on the cold ground under the stars. At night, she searched the sky for stars of the "Drinking Gourd," the Big Dipper, which pointed to the North Star that served as a steady guidepost on the road out of slavery. After many long and weary days of travel, she crossed the northern border of Delaware and passed into the free state of Pennsylvania. Years later, she recalled, "I looked at my hands to see if I was the same person now I was free. There was such a glory over everything, the sun came like gold through the trees, and over the fields, and I felt like I was in heaven."

Harriet Tubman would never again have to call any man "Master," but then came the bitter realization that she was alone and her family remained enslaved. None of them had had the courage to dare what she had done, and unless she made the effort to liberate them, she would never see them again or know their fate. Tubman resolved to do what few successful fugitive slaves ever did. At the risk of recapture and death, she decided to return to Maryland to lead other slaves

Unlike most fugitive slaves who reached the free states, Harriet Tubman returned to Maryland to lead others who were held in bondage to freedom. One of those trips took her up the Nanticoke River past Cannon's Ferry to Seaford. *Courtesy of the Library of Congress.*

across Delaware to freedom. Tubman's decision would earn her the title "Moses." She later recalled, "I had crossed the line of which I had so long been dreaming. I was free; but there was no one to welcome me to the land of freedom. I was a stranger in a strange land, and my home, after all, down in the old cabin quarter, with the old folks and my brothers and sisters. But to this solemn resolution I came; I was free, and they should be free also; I would make a home for them in the North, and the Lord helping me, I would bring them all there."

For the next decade, she would appear some dark night at the door of one of the cabins on a plantation, where a trembling band of fugitives was anxiously awaiting her. She then retraced the route of her own escape, sometimes carrying babies, drugged with paregoric, in a basket on her arm. She carried a revolver to protect herself from anyone who might try to apprehend her. Tubman reasoned, "There was one of two things I had a right to, liberty, or death; if I could not have one, I would have the other; for no man should take me alive; I should fight for my liberty as long as my strength lasted, and when the time for me to go, the Lord would let them take me." Tubman also carried the pistol to silence any of her charges who might turn back. Dead men, according to Tubman, "Tell no tales."

On one of these trips, Tubman's path intersected with the route that Patty Cannon's kidnap victims took decades ago. Tilly, a young slave woman in Maryland, was engaged to be married to a man who was also a slave, but he lived on another plantation. When the man's master discovered that he was going to be sold, he resolved to run away. At first, the plan was that Tilly would join him as he escaped, but she was not able to get away. Tilly's fiancé joined with a group that Tubman successfully led to the North. After seven years, he contacted Tubman and furnished her with some money to rescue Tilly. Tubman, armed with papers that indicated that she was free woman of color and living in Philadelphia, took a steamboat from the Pennsylvania city and traveled through the Chesapeake and Delaware Canal to Baltimore.

After she arrived in Baltimore, and after a considerable search, Tubman located Tilly. Tubman knew that she could not bring a strange woman north from Baltimore to Philadelphia, either by railroad or steamboat, without arousing suspicion, and therefore, Tubman decided on a bold plan. She planned to take Tilly south down the Chesapeake Bay. After a tense moment on the Baltimore docks, Tilly and Tubman boarded a steamboat, crossed the Chesapeake Bay and headed southward. The steamboat entered the Nanticoke River and chugged passed Cannon's Ferry. When the steamboat arrived at Seaford, Tubman and Till went boldly to John L. Colbourn's Hotel in the center of town, ate supper and stayed the night.

On the next morning when they were leaving the hotel, a slave trader attempted to arrest them. Tubman, never flinching, produced the certificate that showed that she was a free person of color from Philadelphia. Colbourn, the hotel manager, intervened, and they were allowed to go. The two women walked a little north of the town to the railroad, boarded the train and continued their journey to freedom.

Tubman's success and her reputation of leading slaves to freedom was so great that slave owners offered a reward of $40,000 for her capture, twenty times the amount offered to apprehend Patty Cannon.

Chapter 4

The Literary Legacy of Patty Cannon

NARRATIVE AND CONFESSIONS OF LUCRETIA P. CANNON

When newspapers reported Patty's arrest and death, the *Delaware Gazette* and the *Niles Weekly Register* reported a summary of her career of crime that was remarkably accurate. It would only be a matter of time before authors would recognize a sensational story that, with a little embellishment, might be a bestseller. Parson Mason Locke Weems, a preacher, writer and traveling book salesman, wrote *The Life and Memorable Actions of George Washington*, which was so popular that the parson turned out a new edition every year or so. In each edition, his imagination reached new heights as he endeavored to show how the life of Washington was an inspiration for Americans of all ages. In the fifth edition, Weems described how young George was scolded by his father for stripping the bark from a cherry tree. According to Weems, George told his father, "I can't tell a lie, Pa; you know I can't tell a lie. I did cut it with my hatchet."

In 1808, Weems visited Lewes, where he heard about a steamy love triangle that involved a doctor, his patient and his patient's wife that ended in the murder of the doctor. He was inspired write a twenty-page pamphlet entitled *God's Revenge Against Adultery*. As he had done with Washington and the cherry tree, Weems embellished the truth in *God's Revenge Against Adultery*, but the pamphlet went through several printings and was a great success.

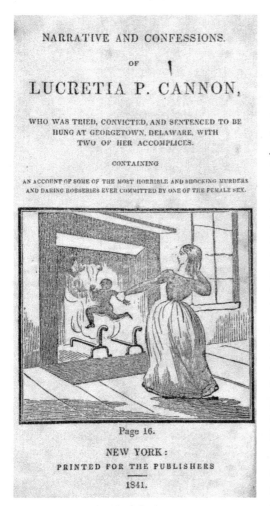

NARRATIVE AND CONFESSIONS.

OF

LUCRETIA P. CANNON,

WHO WAS TRIED, CONVICTED, AND SENTENCED TO BE
HUNG AT GEORGETOWN, DELAWARE, WITH
TWO OF HER ACCOMPLICES.

CONTAINING

AN ACCOUNT OF SOME OF THE MOST HORRIBLE AND SHOCKING MURDERS
AND DARING ROBBERIES EVER COMMITTED BY ONE OF THE FEMALE SEX.

Page 16.

NEW YORK:

PRINTED FOR THE PUBLISHERS

1841.

Published twelve years after her death, the *Narrative and Confessions of Lucretia P. Cannon* promised "an account of some of the most horrible and shocking murders and daring robberies ever committed by one of the female sex."

In 1841, two enterprising authors attempted to do the same when they used Patty Cannon's career to create the *Narrative and Confessions of Lucretia P. Cannon, the Female Murderer.* Published by Clinton Jackson and Erastus E. Barclay, who were assumed to be the authors, the twenty-four-page pamphlet featured a cover picture that was as lurid as nineteenth-century standards would allow. A shapely woman stood with her upper body tilted provocatively to one side. With her back to the viewer and her face toward a blazing fireplace, her right hand kept her long hair in place. As she stood in her "come hither" pose, the woman's left hand was demurely tossing a small child into the roaring fireplace.

The *Narrative and Confessions of Lucretia P. Cannon* told the tale of Patty Cannon, opening with the ominous statement, "It has probably never fallen to the lot of man to record a list of more cruel, heart-rending, atrocious, cold-blooded, and horrible crimes and murders, than have been perpetrated by the subjects of this narrative…in the midst of a highly civilized and Christian community…deeds too, which for the depravity of every human feeling, seem scarcely to have found a parallel in the annals of crime."

As if this were not enough to grab the reader's attention, the *Narrative* went on to state on its opening page, "And it seems doubly shocking, and atrocious, when we find them committed by one of the female sex, which sex has always been esteemed as having higher regard for virtue, and for greater aversion to acts of barbarity, even in the most abandoned of the sex than in generally found in men of the same class. And we may truly say that we have never seen recorded a greater instance of moral depravity so utterly regardless of every feeling which should inhabit the human breast, as the one it becomes our painful lot to lay before our readers in the accounts of Lucretia P. Cannon, the subject of this truly interesting narrative."

Well aware that pamphlets of this nature were prone to exaggeration, the authors of the *Narrative* assured its readers, "And we will now proceed to state the facts as they have actually transpired, and our readers may rely upon the accounts as being correct, as they have been gathered from the most authentic sources." Although the sources are not listed in the *Narrative*, it appears that the authors had access to the newspaper accounts of the crimes of Patty and gang, particularly the reports of Jesse Griffith's execution and those that dealt with the circumstances of Patty's arrest.

With that as an introduction, the *Narrative* launched into Patty's family history. According to the *Narrative*, her father was L.P. Hanly, the son of a wealthy English nobleman from Yorkshire County, England. When Hanly secretly married a woman who lacked social standing but possessed feminine charms in abundance, his family was aghast and summarily disowned him. Fueled by his wife's encouragement and money, Hanley moved to Canada, and for a time, he lived a comfortable, law-abiding life with his wife, four daughters and a son. When Hanly fell on hard times, he joined a gang of smugglers and moved to a little village located on the trade routes to Plattsburg, New York, and Burlington, Vermont.

Hanly apparently had a great deal of success in his nefarious activities when an old acquaintance, Alexander Payne, moved to the same small village. Payne was a frequent visitor to Hanly's house, but he sensed that something was amiss. Passing by Hanly's house one night, he saw Hanly and several other men unloading some goods that Payne believed to be either stolen or smuggled. Confronting Hanly, Payne threatened to go to the authorities, but Hanly pleaded with his friend to give him three days to settle his affairs and leave the country, swearing on all that was holy that he would mind his ways. Payne relented and gave Hanly three days to make do on his promises.

Payne left Hanly that night confident that he had done the right thing. Hanly left that night confident that Payne must die. Summoning members of his smuggling gang, Hanly planned the murder of Payne. Late the next night, the gang, having armed themselves for the deed, met near Payne's house. When the intended victim did not return home, the gang repaired to a nearby tavern to refresh their resolve. When Payne finally returned home, Hanly led his thugs to the house, which they surrounded to intercept Payne should he escape and to give the alarm in case they were discovered. Hanly then entered the house. Moving carefully through the darkened building, Hanly opened the door to the bedroom where Payne and his wife were asleep, Payne, however, was awakened by the sound of the door opening and called out, "Who's there?' Not pausing to answer, Hanly raised an axe and struck Payne in the head, nearly burying the axe to the socket and splitting his old friend's head. Not satisfied that the ghastly wound was fatal, Hanly drew a large butcher's knife, plunged it into his victim's chest and then slit the undoubtedly dead man's throat from ear to ear.

Awakened by the bloody mayhem inflicted upon her husband, Payne's wife began an interminable shrieking. Hanly ignored the distraught woman, but her cries echoed around the neighborhood. Hanly's cohorts showed their mettle by fleeing, but Payne's neighbors responded by apprehending Hanly as he left the house. He was tried, found guilty of murder and executed.

Hanly's widow, with his four daughters and a son, opened a boardinghouse. The son took up with gamblers, drinkers and other low-lifes and developed into what one writer called "a perfect sot." Three of the daughters were able to marry respectable husbands. One day, Jesse Cannon, from western Sussex County, booked a room. When he was staying at the widow Hanly's boardinghouse, Cannon became sick and was nursed back to health by Patty, Hanly's youngest daughter. The two fell in love and were married. Cannon took his young bride back to his home in Sussex County, Delaware.

The *Narrative* devoted over nine pages—nearly half of the pamphlet—to the story of Patty's origins, and it got the booklet off to a rousing start, but it has not been corroborated by contemporary sources, and it may be one of the authors' greatest embellishments in their pamphlet. Another fabrication was the creation of the name "Lucretia" for Patty. Nowhere does this name appear in the historical record. She is almost always styled as "Patty Cannon." Other incidents in the *Narrative*, however, can be verified by newspaper accounts and other documents that date to Patty's time. The pamphlet gave a full and apparently correct account of the ambush of the slave trader Ridgell in 1813. In addition, the *Narrative* included an illustration of the attack on Ridgell and his companion, which was one of the earliest images of one of Patty's crimes.

The *Narrative* also provided uncorroborated details about the attack on a slave trader whose bones were later found near Patty's field. According to the *Narrative*, a slave trader called at Patty's house with two valuable slaves, intending to take them to Norfolk. While at her house, a heavy rainstorm convinced him to stay the night. Patty put him in a room isolated from the main part of the house, and during the night, she entered with a large knotty club and literally beat his brains out. She and some of her gang took the dead man's money, gold watch and slaves, who were locked in a cellar. The murdered man's body was buried in a field near the house under a trash heap. The slaves were confined with little food for a week, until they were taken to the river, where they were sold to a slave dealer who was headed for the South.

In particular, the *Narrative* offered details about the murder of the babies for which she was indicted. Patty supposedly had a rattan switch with a heavy weight fastened at the end, and if any of these young children were troublesome or likely to expose the kidnapping by crying, she would hit them in the head with her switch, killing them. Patty buried these young victims in the cellar or in the field near her house.

According to the *Narrative*, there was a fifteen-year-old African American servant living in Patty's house. Although he had been in her house for nearly a year, she did not trust him and avoided doing anything of a criminal nature while he was present. After she burned and killed the five-year-old, one of the other African Americans told the teenage servant about how she had burned the child to death. The teenager vowed to expose her crime, and he ran away. Unfortunately, Patty saw him leaving the house and suspected something was wrong. She dispatched one of her henchmen to capture the servant. When he was brought back into the house, Patty asked him why he was running away. The teenager admitted that he was going to report her for the murder of the child. Enraged, Patty picked up a large fire shovel and beat him until he was nearly dead. She then took him down to the cellar and locked him among the dead bodies and skeletons of the children she had murdered. Patty left him in that dreadful place for two days without giving him anything to eat or drink. Sleeping on the cold, damp dirt floor, the teenager nearly died before she came down to see if he was still alive. After she brought him some cold food and a little water, she asked him if he would inform against her if she would release him. The servant, forthrightly but foolishly, answered that he would. Patty picked up a rock, beat him to death and left him lying in the cellar to rot.

Most of these stories in the *Narrative*, with the exception of her family origins, have a scintilla of evidence to support them, but many of the details were created by the authors, no doubt to bolster their claim that Patty committed the most "cruel, heart-rending, atrocious, cold-blooded, and horrible crimes and murders." Unlike the pamphlets penned by Parson Weems, the *Narrative and Confessions of Lucretia P. Cannon* did not enjoy much success, and it was left to other authors to bring the life of Patty Cannon to prominence.

THE ENTAILED HAT

Not much is known about Clinton Jackson and Erastus E. Barclay. They may have been the authors of the *Narrative and Confessions of Lucretia P. Cannon*, or they may have been just the publishers of the booklet. In the nineteenth century, George Alfred Townsend, on the other hand, was one of the most prominent newspaper correspondents in America when he wrote the book that brought Patty Cannon lasting fame. At a time when newspapers were the unrivaled sources of information and opinion, Townsend's articles were eagerly read by a nationwide audience. A contemporary commented, "He is known everywhere in the newspaper world and before the American people."

Born in Georgetown on January 30, 1841, his father was the Reverend Stephen Townsend, who served Sussex County as a Methodist clergyman for more than half a century. As a teenager, Townsend demonstrated a talent for writing, and when the Civil War began, he landed a job as a correspondent for the *New York Herald*. Townsend's vivid descriptions of the fighting in Virginia soon earned him a large following. In 1862, the Georgetown native embarked on a lecture tour of Europe, and when he returned to America, his dispatches describing the final days of the Confederacy confirmed his national reputation as a journalist. After President Abraham Lincoln's assassination, Townsend's reports on the Booth conspiracy were an early and important contribution to investigative reporting. His dispatches on the Civil War had won him a national reputation, and after the war, he continued to write about important current events and issues under his nom de plume, "Gath."

In 1867, Townsend stayed at a rooming house with a number of other newspapermen and writers, including Samuel Langhorn Clemens (Mark

Photographed in 1871, three newspapermen in Washington, D.C., *from left to right*: George Alfred Townsend, the author of *The Entailed Hat*; Samuel Longhorn Clemens (Mark Twain); and David Grey, a reporter for the *Buffalo Courier*. *Courtesy of the Library of Congress.*

Twain). Clemens, Townsend and others considered a plan to syndicate their columns by sending duplicates of the same articles to newspapers in different cities, but nothing came of the plan. Lacking a syndicate, Townsend turned out columns at a prodigious rate. An observer described the writer's weekly output:

George Alfred Townsend, otherwise known as "Gath," writes about twenty-one columns a week for the Cincinnati Enquirer, *two for the* Philadelphia Times, *two for the* Boston Globe, *and two or three a week for the* New York Tribune. *He sends three columns daily to the* Cincinnati Enquirer *by telegraph, and his income from the aggregate of his newspaper work is thought not to fall below £10,000 a year. He keeps two assistants, one of whom takes down his dictation in shorthand, while the other does the writing out.*

In addition to his newspaper dispatches, the indefatigable Townsend wrote poetry, biographies and novels, which were often a blend of historical fact and fiction.

In 1880, Townsend was invited to speak at the Independence Day celebration at Georgetown, and he wrote a poem based on the historic ride of Caesar Rodney, a Delaware delegate to the Continental Congress who had cast a critical vote on the Declaration of Independence. Rodney had left the Congress to help suppress a Tory uprising in southern Delaware when the question of independence came up for a vote. Rodney's hasty return to Philadelphia was an ingrained part of Delaware lore, but Townsend decided to give the historical facts a romantic twist in his poem "Caesar Rodney's Fourth of July, 1776." According to Townsend, a fetching Tory, Sarah Rowland, "widow, witty, wealthy, fine," amused Rodney until the vote was taken. As the Georgetown poet put it, after Rodney discovered that he was needed in Philadelphia, he called for his horse and scampered across Sussex County on his way to Philadelphia, where he was greeted by Thomas McKean, the other Delaware delegate who supported independence: "Down the street a hot horse stumbled, and a man in riding frock, with a green patch on his visage, and his garments white with grime. 'Now, praise God!' McKean spoke grimly, 'Caesar Rodney is on time.'" Townsend concluded his address with stirring words, "Here this day is made a nation by the help of Delaware!"

The inspiring lines of "Caesar Rodney's Fourth of July, 1776" make great reading, but unfortunately, Townsend's poetic license had run amuck. As William Frank demonstrated in his booklet *Caesar Rodney Patriot*, the Sarah Rowland story was a complete fabrication. Townsend's independence as a writer had triumphed over his judgment as a historian. Four years after Townsend delivered his fanciful poem in Georgetown, he published his hallmark novel, *The Entailed Hat, or Patty Cannon's Times, A Romance*. While researching his mother's ancestors in the Worcester County Court House in

Snow Hill, Townsend stumbled onto a will in which a man left his son "my best hat...and no more of my estate." The bequest of a hat, and no more, sparked an idea for a book that blended the historical facts of Patty's crimes with a fictional story of a Delmarva ironmaster.

In *The Entailed Hat*, Townsend recounted many of the crimes of Patty Cannon and demonstrated that he was familiar with the newspaper accounts of her activities and the *Narrative and Confessions of Lucretia P. Cannon*. Townsend's description of the sinister Patty Cannon became the late nineteenth-century face of the southern Delaware felon: "She was what is called a 'chunky' woman, short and thick, with rosy skin, low but pleasing forehead, coal-black hair, a rolling way of swaying and moving herself, a pair of large black eyes at once daring, furtive, and familiar, and a large neck and large breast, uniting the bulldog and the dam, cruelty and full womanhood."

In one incident, he attempted to capture the essence of her character. After flirting with a slave trader who had with him a great deal of money, Townsend described Patty as she went to the trader's bedroom and knocked. Eagerly the slave trader opened the door and

> *as he made one step to penetrate the darkness with his dazzled eyes, Patty Cannon silently thrust against his heart a huge horse-pistol and pulled the trigger: a flash of fire from the sharp flint against the fresh powder in the pan lift up the hall an instant, and the heavy body of the guest fell backward before his chair, and over him leaned the woman a moment, still as death, with the heavy pistol clubbed, ready to strike if he should stir.*
>
> *He did not move, but only bled at the large lips, ghastly and unprotesting, and the cold blue eyes looked as natural as life.*
>
> *Patty Cannon took the chair and counted the money.*

All of the principal people in Patty's life were portrayed in *The Entailed Hat*, including the Johnson brothers and Cyrus James. Townsend also included a description of Patty's cousins, the loan sharks Isaac and Jacob Cannon. According to Townsend, the brothers' warehouse could hardly hold the vast aggregate of pots and kettles, spinning wheels and cradles, bedsteads and beds, harrows and ploughs, chairs and gridirons, rakes and hoes, silhouettes and picture frames, handmade quilts of calico and pillows of home-plucked geese feathers, fishermen's nets and oars—whatever made the substance of living in an old country without minerals and manufactures in the early part of the nineteenth century."

When a character asks why the brothers kept all of these things rotting away in storage, Townsend had one of the Cannons reply: "We keep em' to show all who trespass on Isaac and Jacob Cannon...that this is a judgment day!"

Two of characters in *The Entailed Hat* were given fictional names, but it appears that Townsend based them on real people. In the book, Sampson Hat, a free man of color, worked as a servant to Meshach Milburn, the operator of an ironworks. Historians believe that Townsend based these two fictional characters on Sampson Harmon and Thomas A. Spence. Harmon was born a slave in the late eighteenth century. Thomas Spence was the owner of a Maryland ironworks, and Harmon worked for him as his personal servant. Following the demise of the ironworks in the middle of the nineteenth century, Harmon lived in a small cabin with his cat, Tom. Townsend portrayed Sampson Hat as a man who "cooked his master's food and performed rough work around the store, but had no other known qualifications for a confidential servant except his bodily power. He was now old, probably sixty, but still a most formidable pugilist, and he had caught, running afoot, the last wild deer in the county."

When *The Entailed Hat* was published, many Delmarva residents recognized Sampson Harmon as the model for the character in Townsend's book. Born in 1790, Harmon had been the free servant to an ironmaster. After the ironworks were closed, Harmon moved into a small cabin in the woods near Snow Hill, Maryland, where he lived

Sampson Harmon, who was believed to be the inspiration for the character "Sampson Hat" in George Alfred Townsend's novel *The Entailed Hat*, depicted on a late nineteenth-century postcard. *Photograph courtesy of the Julia A. Purnell Museum.*

with a large black cat named Tom. Once the book was published, Harmon's neighbors began calling him "Sampson Hat." He eventually moved to the Worcester County Poor House Farm, where he posed for photographs and died in 1898.

The Entailed Hat was published in 1884, and the book was immediately popular. Townsend's book went through several printings, and the novel marked the pinnacle of his career. Although he continued to write for another two decades after the publication of *The Entailed Hat*, his popularity began to decline. By the start of the twentieth century, Townsend had developed diabetes, and the combination of his failing health and changing public taste made it difficult for the Sussex author to earn a living. At one point, Townsend was forced to sell books from his library to pay his bills. In 1911, an old friend, the Wilmington industrialist Samuel Bancroft Jr., offered to underwrite the publication of an anthology of Townsend's poems. Two years later, *Poems of the Delaware Peninsula* was published, but only a few copies were sold. Unlike his friend Mark Twain, when Townsend died in 1914, he had been virtually forgotten by the American public.

Part of the restored ironworks in Furnace Town near Snow Hill, Maryland. The ironworks in central Delmarva employed a mixed labor force of white and black workers and were a critical part of the setting of George Alfred Townsend's *The Entailed Hat*. *Photo by Michael Morgan.*

After World War II, Temple University graduate student Ruthanna Hindes wrote her master's thesis on Townsend, which was later published as a book. In 1950, the University of North Carolina Press reprinted some of Townsend's Civil War writings, and in 1955, Tidewater Publishers reprinted *The Entailed Hat*. More recently, in 2000, Nanticoke Books published a slightly modernized version of Townsend's novel. The new edition of *The Entailed Hat* was edited by Hal Roth, who modified spelling, punctuation and sentence structure to make the novel more appealing to the twenty-first-century reader.

PATTY CANNON LIVE!

Forefront in the resurgence of interest in George Alfred Townsend and Patty Cannon following World War II was Ashworth Burslem's 1951 play with the simple title *Patty Cannon*. Burslem, assistant city editor of the *Wilmington Journal–Every Evening*, fashioned a three-act play based on the notorious killer that was produced by the Wilmington Drama League as a workshop presentation. Burslem's drama depicted Cannon as "feared by every free-born Negro in Delaware, hated by everyone with a sense of justice, tolerated by the majority who approved of her results, and loved by one man."

According to the *Journal–Every Evening*, Burslem's play depicted a woman who would murder at the slightest provocation, but who would tenderly care for the flowers that grew in the wall box of her home. The play showed Patty "lashing out with equal sting and accuracy whether using her whip or tongue[.] She has one of the most lawless band of rogues ever assembled under one roof cowering at her command."

To further soften the image of Patty, Burslem invented a completely fictional character, Pierre Laudain, "a Frenchman with a glamorous past and a smooth tongue," to serve as Patty's love interest. Phyllis Wood Anderson played Patty, and according to the *Journal–Every Evening*, "given a part that requires her to run the gamut of emotions, Mrs. Anderson makes the relentlessness of Patty Cannon real, and terrifying." Not only was the role of Patty emotionally demanding, but it was also physically challenging. As Patty, Anderson "wrestles a New York stranger into submission, wraps her whip around arm or neck with equal dexterity, and kills the man she loves with the same ease that she murders a wealthy stranger."

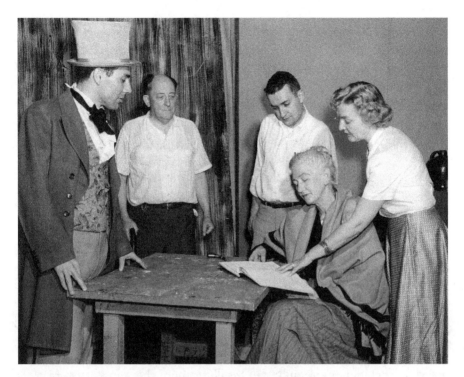

A production that dealt with the career of Patty Cannon was presented in 1955. *From left to right*: Ernest Sutton, M. Bader, Richard Evans, Charlotte Hansen and Elizabeth Kase. *Courtesy of the Delaware Public Archives.*

After its initial presentation in Wilmington, Burslem's play was performed at Laurel High School in April 1952. Reprising her role as Delmarva's most notorious criminal, Anderson thrilled the packed auditorium, despite what some saw as historical anachronism. Gilbert S. Jones, reviewing the play for the *Laurel State Register*, pointed out that Anderson's long, voluminous hair was more in keeping with a twentieth-century movie star than a woman between sixty and seventy years of age who looked like a man. Despite these inaccuracies, the 1,400 people who attended the performances in Laurel were thoroughly engaged in Anderson's performance. A member of the audience was reported to exclaim, "She was a bad woman. I never liked a bad woman." When another theater patron was told that the drama group was staying in the Laurel homes, she remarked, "Thank heavens that woman, Patty Cannon, is not going to stay in my home tonight."

The audience in Laurel generally approved of the portrayal of Patty in Burslem's play, but they may not have appreciated the depiction of the Delmarva kidnapper and killer in the April 1954 edition of the men's magazine *Cavalier*. Patty was the central figure in a fictionalized story entitled "The Case of the Sobbing Owl," by William Hartley (who wrote a number of short stories for men's magazines based on historical events). Under the headline, "By day beautiful Patty Hanley killed her guests with kindness. By night she just plain killed them," Patty was depicted as having "acquired a fierce autocratic air" as she grew older, and the story said, "it had become her habit to wear men's clothing and to carry a heavily weighted riding crop. She was carrying it now, and she slapped it furiously against her boots."

Hartley described Patty as being as powerful as a man, and she would often challenge men to wrestling matches during which she would sometimes throw her opponent across the length of the tavern floor. According to Hartley, "The neighboring farmers called her Terrible Patty Cannon, and feared her as they feared the devil."

Hartley was writing a fictional story for a publication whose readers wanted a sensationalized tale. "The Case of the Sobbing Owl" was illustrated by Howell Dodd, who imposed a mid-twentieth-century voyeurism on his portrayal of the Delmarva criminal. Dodd, a prolific illustrator (who sometimes worked under differed pseudonyms in the same publication), was noted for including more nudity in his illustrations that most artists of that time. Some of Dodd's stories included titles such as "Rome's Naked Girl Gladiators" and "The Nude in the Blue Lagoon," which featured illustrations as uninhibited as the titles suggested. The title panel of "The Case of the Sobbing Owl" featured a two-page spread that showed a cutaway of Patty's house. On the ground floor, Patty, whose dress is in disarray, was being threatened by a dark-haired man brandishing a whip. In the attic, over a half-dozen African Americans of various ages—including an old man praying, a woman nursing a baby and others—are shown in shackles. In another illustration, Patty is depicted as a slender woman with close cropped-hair and dressed in a loose blouse, tight pants and tall boots. "The Case of the Sobbing Owl" may have introduced Patty Cannon to new readers, but it is doubtful that they would have recognized the true Delmarva killer had they met her.

Chapter 5
Along the Nanticoke

WHERE PATTY WALKED

In the years after Patty died, the landscape where she lived and committed her crimes changed greatly. Steamboats began to schedule regular runs out of Seaford, and that brought social changes to the Nanticoke. In 1854, the *Osiris* began carrying passengers between Seaford and Baltimore. The steamer ran to Baltimore twice a week, and on other days, it ran day trips down the Nanticoke River to the Chesapeake Bay. Sussex County native William Morgan, who described the deaths of Jacob and Isaac Cannon, took one of the excursion cruises aboard the *Osiris* and noted in his diary, "I went on an excursion in the steamboat *Osiris* down to Deal's Island, very pleasant day. Had on board 300. It was jovial time to be sure. They had a brass band of music. Some say a cotillion band, and how some danced, some kicked and capered on the hurricane deck, all looked on that wished to."

Morgan was a devout Methodist, and he found great temptations aboard the steamboat: "I was nearer a dance, perhaps than I had been for half a century on which I looked not. Some sung hymns and spiritual songs below, or in the saloon. On the forward part of the deck were the whiskey suckers and rowdies, but few of them made their appearance in the saloon. We returned home about 11 o'clock p.m., weary and tired."

The popularization of steamboats made another change on the towns along the Nanticoke. In the nineteenth century, Laurel, Seaford and other small riverfront communities had boatyards that turned out sloops, schooners and other sailing craft. Some of the schooners built in Sussex County were larger than the steam vessels that plied Delaware waters, but the towns in the southern part of the state lacked the machine shops necessary to build steam engines. Consequently, the steamers were built at Baltimore, Wilmington and other large cities, and the boatyards on the Nanticoke and its tributaries began a steady decline.

Two years after Morgan took an excursion on the *Osiris*, the indefatigable diarist noted, "The rail road [*sic*] cars passengers train came down for the first time to Seaford. The longed [*sic*] looked for rail road has reach its terminus on this day, Sunday, [November] 30th. The men worked hard to get the turn table [*sic*] set; now the locomotive for the first time turned on it about 4 o'clock p.m." It once took the schooner of Joe Johnson a week to reach Philadelphia, but now the trip from Seaford to the Pennsylvania city could now be made in a matter of hours, and Morgan gave his blessing: "Success to the enterprise. Amen."

In the 1850s, the tracks were laid through Seaford and Laurel to Delmar, and the changes in these towns was almost immediate. In 1857, Morgan noted, "The people seem in a mania for lots in Seaford."

As the towns of central Delmarva grew, the places, buildings and streets that Patty, Joe Johnson and the other gang members frequented were altered or

Patty as depicted in the Seaford Historical Society Museum as part of a large-scale diorama of the front of her house. *Photo by Michael Morgan.*

torn down and replaced. The Seaford Historical Society, however, maintains an excellent eleven-thousand-square-foot museum in the center of town on High Street. Among other exhibits related to the history of the area is an exhibit of Patty Cannon as she sits in a rocking chair on the porch of her house. Nearby, in Gateway Park, at the corner of High and North Market Streets, is a historical marker commemorating Harriet Tubman's successful efforts to rescue the slave Tilly on the Underground Railroad. In the Seaford museum, that story is told right after the Patty Cannon exhibit. The Seaford Historical

A close-up of Patty's face in the Seaford Historical Society Museum does not show the weathered and wrinkled skin of a woman who was about sixty or seventy years old. *Photo by Michael Morgan.*

Society was also instrumental in having Seaford designated as part of the National Park Service's Network to Freedom for the research completed by museum curator Jim Blackwell in documenting the Tilly escape. The Seaford Museum is also part of the National Park Service's Chesapeake Bay Gateway Network and the Captain John Smith National Historic Trail.

The arrival of the railroad at Georgetown in 1868 spurred the construction of sawmills, factories, canneries and other businesses, which allowed the town to develop into a commercial as well as a governmental center. The county seat has outgrown the boundaries that were laid out in the late eighteenth century, but in spite of the construction that occurred in the nineteenth and twentieth centuries, government buildings still circle the square in the center of town. In 1879, the courthouse where Patty and Joe Johnson were taken when they were arrested was sold to make room for a new building. The original structure was moved to its present location on a side street when a new building was constructed. The old courthouse now sits on South Bedford Street and was once used as a private residence and

The eighteenth-century courthouse that was erected in Georgetown shortly after the town was established and was in use during Patty's lifetime. *Photo by Michael Morgan.*

The interior of the restored old Georgetown courthouse where the case against Joe Johnson would have been heard and where the trial of Patty Cannon would have been held had she not died in jail. *Photo by Michael Morgan.*

a print shop. A major renovation was completed in 1976, and the building appears as it was when Patty was arrested.

Next to the old courthouse, an example of a whipping post was erected to serve as a reminder of Delaware justice in former years. During the nineteenth century, most states abandoned corporal punishment of criminals, but the whipping post remained an entrenched feature of the Delaware legal system. In 1873, the *New York Times* reported, "Corporal punishment is an important feature of the Delaware penal code. For instance, whipping is a part of the punishment of all minor degrees of murder, and for burglary, mayhem, violent assault, kidnapping, highway robbery, attempted poisoning, arson, larceny, counterfeiting, and other felonies and misdemeanors." The number of lashes administered ranged from twenty to sixty, and, in general, the whipped person also had to spend an hour in the pillory. Forgery, perjury, fortune-telling, conspiracy and other offenses were punishable only by a stay in the pillory.

Many in Delaware saw the whipping post and the pillory as being essential to maintaining law and order in the state. According to a nineteenth-century Delaware newspaper:

> *We should not, did time and space permit, waste a moment on the merits of that effective and invaluable judicial weapon—the whipping post. The satisfactory results speak loudly for themselves; and the absence in our courts of the class of criminals, known as "old offenders," together with the proportional annual reduction of crime in the community, declares that its terrors are rarely brought into requisition the second time for the benefit of the same convict...The pillory and whipping post need no defense in Delaware from Delawareans.*

By the beginning of the twentieth century, the whipping post and pillory had begun to fall out of favor, but the floggings continued. During the Great Depression, five men in southern Delaware were convicted of stealing chickens and other minor crimes. In February 1932, the five were sentenced to the whipping post, and the punishment was carried out in Georgetown. According to the *Delaware Coast News*, "More than two thousand people, men, women, and children, some of the women with babies in their arms stood crowded about the wire enclosure surrounding the new Sussex County Jail, located at the Almshouse farm two miles from Georgetown Saturday afternoon, in a chilly February wind, waiting from 10 o'clock until 1:30." After the whippings in Georgetown, the last flogging in Delaware occurred

The whipping post remained a part of the Delaware justice system well into the twentieth century. *Courtesy of the Delaware Public Archives.*

in 1952, and the practice that had its roots in a medieval sense of justice was formally abandoned twenty years later.

Despite the industrial growth in some towns on Delmarva (a nylon factory was built in Seaford just prior to World War II), along the Nanticoke there are places that are as serene and natural as they were in Patty's time. After the death of Isaac and Jacob Cannon, the ferry passed into the hands of their heirs, and the name was changed to the Woodland Ferry in the late nineteenth century. The General Assembly declared that the ferry should be free of charge and operate from dawn to dusk. The ferry consisted of a scow that was poled across the river, and in 1930, a Model "T" engine was attached to the ferryboat to propel it across the river. The Delaware State Highway Division took over the ferry in 1935, and it continues to operate the short, pleasant ride as part of the highway system. The crossing takes about four or five minutes. On the northwest side of the river is a small cemetery where Jacob and Isaac Cannon are buried. A few hundred yards away is Cannon Hall, which suffered a destructive fire in 2010, but efforts are being made to restore the building.

Cannon's Ferry, renamed Woodland Ferry, in operation in the middle of the twentieth century. The two-story building in the background to the right is Cannon Hall. The cemetery with the graves of Isaac and Jacob Cannon are out of the picture to the left. *Courtesy of the Delaware Public Archives.*

Cannon Hall in the process of being rebuilt after a devastating fire in 2010 that gutted most of the building. *Photo by Michael Morgan.*

Reliance, Maryland, formerly Johnson's Crossroads, where Johnson's Tavern once stood. The road from Cannon's Ferry is at the bottom of the picture. The Delaware border is on the right side of the image. *Photo by Michael Morgan.*

This building in Reliance (formerly Johnson's Crossroads) was once thought to be Patty's house. *Photo by Michael Morgan.*

After research indicated that this building was most likely constructed after Patty's death, the words "NEARBY STOOD" were painted on the marker. *Photo by Michael Morgan.*

Just a few miles up Woodland Ferry Road is Reliance, formerly Johnson's Crossroads, where a historical marker erected in 1939 by the state of Maryland stands in front of a wood-frame building. The embossed text on the marker reads, "PATTY CANNON'S HOUSE At Johnson's Crossroads where the noted kidnapping group had headquarters as described in George Alfred Townsend's novel, 'The Entailed Hat'. The house borders on Caroline and Dorchester counties and the state of Delaware." After the marker was erected, further research revealed that the building was erected after Patty had died. In view of this research, the Maryland State Roads Commission had the words "NEARBY STOOD" painted on the sign.

A few hundred yards away and across the Delaware-Maryland border is another historical marker that was erected by the state of Delaware. This marker, erected in 2012, summarizes the activities of the Cannon-Johnson kidnapping gang and is dedicated to "the victims of this evil enterprise, and those who struggled against it."

The location of Johnson's Tavern and Patty Cannon's house has been a puzzle that no one has definitively solved. Her house is often described as being on the Delaware-Maryland line and within a stone's throw of the boundary between Dorchester and Carolina Counties in Maryland. The

In the distance is the likely location of Patty's house. The road running across the center of the picture is on the Delaware-Maryland border, and the boundary between Dorchester and Caroline Counties in Maryland is just off the right side of the image. *Photo by Michael Morgan.*

The most likely candidate for Patty's house. This photo was taken in the late 1940s by William Handy and shows members of the Handy family. *From left to right*: Irv, Billy, Mrs. Handy and Jane Ann. The building was demolished a few years after this picture was taken. *Courtesy of Irv Handy and the Seaford Historical Society.*

tavern, which was at Johnson's Crossroads (Reliance), was also described as being near Patty's house. The boundaries between the two states and the two Maryland counties converge a few miles north of Reliance. It may all come down to what "nearby" means. The most likely candidate for Patty Cannon's house is the building that was once owned by the Handy family. The building once sat on the Maryland-Delaware border north of Reliance, but in the first part of the twentieth century, it was moved and turned into a storage building. The house was unique in that the upper rooms were separated by a wall and each could be entered only by its individual staircase. The building was torn down several years after World War II.

The Skull That Harbored a Criminal Mind

When Patty Cannon died, whether by poison or natural causes, in the Georgetown jail, her earthly remains were supposedly interred in the yard next to the jail. At least, the major part of her body was buried. The brothers Lorenzo Niles and Orson Squire Fowler, two of the leading phrenologists of the early nineteenth century, were on a lecture tour in Maryland Delaware when they learned of Patty's career of crime. Phrenologists studied the irregularities in the shape of the skull to determine the character and personality traits of a person. In the early nineteenth century, phrenologists believed that the multiple functions of the brain were distinct and were located in a separate area of the brain. It was believed that the size of that section of the brain indicated the intensity of that particular function, and the shape of the skull was determined by the size of the area of the various functions. Some phrenologists felt the head of the patient with their hands, while others used calibers and measuring tapes to chart the hills and valleys of the skull and compare it to charts that mapped the traits, such as combativeness, adhesiveness (attachment to others) and amativeness (romantic love or lust).

While on their lecture tour, the Fowler brothers somehow acquired Patty's skull. The phrenologists put it on display in their New York museum and included a description of it in the *Phrenological Journal* in 1840 and the *Phrenological Almanac* in 1841. The authors of the *Narrative and Confessions of Patty Cannon* mentioned the acquisition of Patty's skull by the phrenologists in their "Concluding Remarks." In 1844, O.S. Fowler wrote in *Education and Self-Improvement*, "A predominance of the propensities and intellect over the

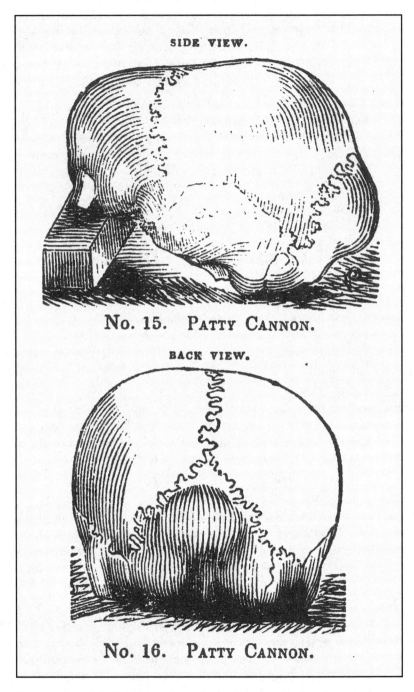

SIDE VIEW.

No. 15.   PATTY CANNON.

BACK VIEW.

No. 16.   PATTY CANNON.

Patty's supposed skull that was drawn in detail and studied by phrenologists in the nineteenth century. From *Hereditary Descent: Its Laws and Facts Applied to Human Improvement.*

moral faculties, leads to most disastrous consequences; for powerful animal desires will then employ a powerful intellect to effect purely selfish, wicked ends, and stop at no means of attaining them. This was the organization of Patty Cannon...and is that of most of the outrages of mankind." Four years later, the *American Phrenological Journal* listed a plaster cast made from her skull and the comment "Patty Cannon, Murderess—All the Moral organs small. The Intellectual, Animal and Domestic organs, very large."

In 1857, O.S. Fowler published a fuller analysis of Patty's skull in *Hereditary Descent: Its Laws and Facts Applied to Human Improvement.* According to Folwer, "This notorious woman shed human blood as lavishly as if it had been water. She procured and held in subjection a desperate gang, whose sole business was to perpetrate the robberies and murders she planned, in which she generally took the lead, and frequently perpetrated murders single handed in order to rob." The reason for this behavior was that "Her Destructiveness, and also Acquistiveness, as well as Amativeness, were enormous."

Patty's skull was apparently not the only skull that the Fowler brothers acquired on their trip through Delmarva. They also obtained the skull of Patty's sister Betty (Betsey) and that of Ebenezer Johnson. Betty's skull indicated that "her Amativeness and Destructiveness, like those of her sister Patty, were extraordinarily developed...The resemblance of these skulls to each other is striking."

O.S. Fowler was not shy about making diagnoses about people whose skulls he did not have. He wrote, "The mother of these depraved women was large and fleshy, and good-natured, yet accused of manifesting undue Amativeness. This passion she transmitted to her daughters, who inherited also their Destructiveness from their father, and hence their wantonness, revengefulness and murderous ferocity."

The skulls that the Fowler brothers obtained on Delmarva were displayed in their museum for many years, and George Alfred Townsend saw them before he wrote *The Entailed Hat.* In his description of the death of Ebenezer Johnson, Townsend wrote, "[Joe King], as he whirled past, grasped the long rifle, drew it to his shoulder, and...put the two balls in that old man's brain. Both balls entered over the left eyebrow." To bolster the veracity of this account, for which there is no known documentation, Townsend included this footnote, "The skull of Ebenezer Johnson can be seen at Folwer & Wells' Museum, New York, with the bullet hole through it. There, also are the skulls of Patty and Betty Cannon."

After *The Entailed Hat* was released, a review in the *Phrenological Journal* compared the book favorably to *Uncle Tom's Cabin* and, referring to the

The skull retrieved from the Georgetown jail yard and put on display at the Dover Public Library. The subject of the portrait is not known. *Courtesy of the Delaware Public Archives.*

subtitle of Townsend's book, went on to comment, "The publishers of the *Phrenological Journal* find in *Patty Cannon's Times*, as revealed in this book, additional interest in the fact that for more than forty years the skulls of Patty and Betsey and Ebenezer Johnson have been preserved in the Phrenological

Museum in New York." What happened to the skulls of Patty and the others when the phrenological museum closed is not known.

Around the beginning of the twentieth century, Patty's remains and those of one or two others were exhumed from the Georgetown jail yard to be properly buried in a cemetery. When the bones were dug up, deputy sheriff James Marsh took what he believed was Patty's skull. A few years later, Marsh gave the skull to Charles I. Joseph, who first hung it on a rafter in his barn and later put in a box and stored in the attic of his house. Eventually, it was passed on to his son Alfred W. Joseph, who kept it for fifteen years before turning it over to the Dover Public Library in 1961. The library stored the skull in a hatbox, but it would be occasionally displayed and shown to people who inquired about it. How the skull got from Fowler and Wells's Museum in New York back into the grave in the Georgetown jail yard has never been explained. Like the location of Patty's house and the circumstances of her death, the history of her skull may never be known, which would not be surprising for the Delmarva woman who struck terror along the Nanticoke.

Bibliography

Abrams, Alan, ed. *Black and Free: The Free Negro in America, 1830*. Sylvania, OH: Doubting Thomas Publishing, 2001.

American Art Archives. "Howell Dodd." http://www.americanartarchives. com/dodd.htm.

American National Biography. "Patty Cannon." http://www.anb.org/ articles/20/20-91919-print.html.

Archives of Maryland Online. Vol. 28. http://aomol.msa.maryland.gov/ html/index.html.

Ball, Charles. *Slavery in the United States: A Narrative of the Life and Adventures of Charles Ball, A Black Man*. Pittsburgh, PA: John S. Taylor, 1837.

Baltimore (MD) Niles Weekly Register, April 25, 1829; May 23, 1829.

Berlin, Ira. *Slaves Without Masters: The Free Negro in the Antebellum South*. New York: New Press, 2007.

Blockson, Charles. *The Underground Railroad, Dramatic Firsthand Accounts of Daring Escapes to Freedom*. New York: Berkley Books, 1987.

Bradford, Sarah. *Harriet, The Moses of Her People*. New York: Geo. R. Lockwood and Son, 1897.

Bready, James H. "Maryland's Own Lucrezia Borgia." *Sun Magazine*, April 3, 1955.

Clark, Charles B. *The Eastern Shore of Maryland Virginia*. New York: Lewis Historical Publishing Company, 1950.

Clayton, John M. Letters, General Reference—Biographies (John M. Clayton). Delaware Public Archives, Dover, Delaware.

Collins, Winfield H. *The Domestic Slave Trade of the Southern States*. New York: Broadway Publishing Company, 1904.

Comegy, Joseph P. "John M. Clayton." *Papers of the Historical Society of Delaware*. Vol. 4. Wilmington: Historical Society of Delaware, 1882.

Crosland, Philip F. "Patty Cannon Drama Clicks," *Wilmington (DE) Journal–Every Evening*, November 2, 1951.

Cuffee, Paul. *Memoir of Captain Paul Cuffee, a Man of Color*. New York: C. Peacock, 1811.

Delaware Department of Transportation. "Woodland Ferry: Crossing the Nanticoke River from the 1740s to the Present." http://www.deldot.gov/archaeology/woodland_ferry/pdf/woodland_ferry_brochure.pdf.

(Dover) Delaware Register, May 1838, vol. 1, no. 4.

Easton Gazette and Eastern Shore Intelligencer, August 19, 1820; July 23, 1821; May 25, 1822.

The Encyclopedia of Great Philadelphia, Philadelphia and Its People in Maps: the 1790s. http://philadelphiaencyclopedia.org/archive/philadelphia-and-its-people-in-maps-the-1790s/.

Federal Writers' Project. *Delaware: A Guide to the First State*. New York: Viking Press, 1938.

Footner, Hulbert. *Rivers of the Eastern Shore, Seventeen Maryland Rivers.* Centreville, MD: Tidewater Publishers, 1972.

Fowler, O.S. *American Phrenological Journal* 7, no. 8 (August 1845).

———. *American Phrenological Journal* 79, no. 4 (October 1884).

———. *Education and Self-Improvement, Founded on Physiology and Phrenology.* New York: O.S. and L.N. Fowler, 1844.

———. *Hereditary Descent: Its Laws and Facts Applied to Human Improvement.* New York: Fowlers and Wells, 1857.

Frank, William P. *Caesar Rodney Patriot.* Wilmington, DE: American Revolution Bicentennial Commission, 1975.

Giles, Ted. "Patty Cannon House a Curiosity Surrounded by Legends of Crime." *Delaware State News*, October 23, 1968.

———. *Patty Cannon, Woman of Mystery.* Easton, MD: Easton Publishing Company, 1965.

Hancock, Harold B. "William Morgan's Autobiography and Diary: Life in Sussex County, 1780–1857." *Delaware History* 19, no. 1 (Spring-Summer 1980).

———. "William Yates's Letter of 1837: Slavery, and Colored People in Delaware." *Delaware History* 14, no. 3 (April 1971).

Harr, Dorothy N. *The Story of a Lost Village: Furnace Town.* Snow Hill, MD: Furnace Town Foundation, 1983.

Hazzard, Robert. *History of Seaford.* Seaford, DE: privately printed, 1899.

History Channel. "Fugitive Slave Acts."

http://www.history.com/topics/black-history/fugitive-slave-acts.

History Detectives. "The Capital: Jack and Rose's House Federalsburg, Maryland." http://www-tc.pbs.org/opb/historydetectives_old/pdf/104_house.pdf.

Hopper, Matthew S. "From Refuge To Strength: The Rise of the African American Church in Philadelphia, 1787–1949." https://www.preservationalliance.com/files/aachurches.pdf.

Horle, Craig, ed. *Records of the Sussex County Delaware, 1677–1710.* Philadelphia: University of Pennsylvania Press, 1991.

Historic American Building Survey. "Cannon Hall (Jacob Cannon House) Woodland, Seaford Hundred, Sussex County, Delaware." Philadelphia: National Park Service, 1960. http://lcweb2.loc.gov/master/pnp/habshaer/de/de0100/de0130/data/de0130data.pdf.

———. "Walnut Landing (A House) on the Nanticoke River, Woodland (formerly Cannons' Ferry) Sussex County Delaware." Philadelphia: National Park Service, 1960. http://lcweb2.loc.gov/master/pnp/habshaer/de/de0100/de0191/data/de0191data.pdf.

Jones, Gilbert S. "Laurel Audiences Have Good Theatre in *Patty Cannon*." *Laurel (MD) State Register*, April 11, 1952.

Little Owl (Charles C. Clark IV). *The Nanticoke, Heartland of Del-Mar-Va.* Georgetown, DE: Sunshine, 1987.

Macdonald, Betty Harrington. "A Sussex County Slave on Board the Schooner *Baraco*." *The Archeolog* 27 (Fall 1976).

Messenger, R.W. *Patty Cannon Administers Justice; Or, Joe Johnson's Last Kidnapping Exploit.* Centreville, MD: Tidewater Publishers, 1960.

Miller, M. Sammy. "Patty Cannon: Murderer and Kidnapper of Free Blacks: A Review of the Evidence." *Maryland Historical Magazine* 72, no. 3. (Fall 1977).

Morgan, Edmund S. *American Slavery American Freedom: The Ordeal of Colonial Virginia.* New York: W.W. Norton and Company, Inc., 1975

Mullin, Gerald W. *Flight and Rebellion.* New York: Oxford University Press, 1972.

"Multilingual Archive, Anthony Johnson (American Colonial)." http://www.worldlingo.com/ma/enwiki/en/Anthony_Johnson_(American_Colonial).

"Negroes Kidnapped." General Reference No. 706, Delaware Public Archives, Dover.

New York Times. April 21, 1869; December 11, 1873.

Obituary Addresses on the Occasion of the Death of the Hon. John M. Clayton of Delaware. Washington, DC: A.G.P. Nicholson, Public Printer, 1857.

Pennsylvania—An Act for the Gradual Abolition of Slavery, 1780. Yale Law School, the Avalon Project. http://avalon.law.yale.edu/18th_century/pennst01.asp.

Philadelphia African Observer. May 1827, July 1827, August 1827 and October 1827.

Pippin, Kathryn. "Patty Cannon, The Eastern Shore's First Lady of Crime." *Shore Living Magazine*, February 2003.

Pray, Lewis G. *Boston Sunday School Hymn Book.* Boston: Sunday School Society, Benjamin H. Greene, 1834.

(Rehoboth Beach) Delaware Coast News. February 10, 1932.

"The Revival of the Whipping Post." *Current Literature* 17 (January–June 1899).

Rollo, Vera F. *Maryland Personality Parade.* Lantham, MD: Maryland Historical Press, 1967.

Roth, Hal. "Fact, Fiction Hard to Separate in Patty Cannon Legend." *Wilmington (DE) Sunday Star*, February 2, 2002.

———. *In Days Gone By and Other Tales from Delmarva.* Vienna, MD: Nanticoke Books, 2002.

———. *The Monster's Handsome Face.* Vienna, MD: Nanticoke Books, 1998.

Schuyler, Montgomery. "A Neglected American Poet." *North American Review*, May 1900.

Seaford (DE) Leader. October 17, 1968.

Shields, Jerry. *Gath's Literary Work and Folk*. Wilmington, DE: Heritage Press, 1996.

Siebert, Wilbur H. *The Underground Railroad from Slavery to Freedom*. New York: Macmillan Company, 1899.

Slavery in the North. "Slavery in Delaware." http://slavenorth.com/delaware.htm.

Smith, Captain John. *The Generall Historie of Virginia, New England and the Summer Isles*. Glasgow: James MacLehose and Sons, 1907.

Smith, Eric Ledell. "Rescuing African American Kidnapping Victims in Philadelphia as Documented in the Joseph Watson Papers at the Historical Society of Pennsylvania." *Pennsylvania Magazine of History and Biography* 129, no. 3 (July 2005). https://journals.psu.edu/pmhb/article/viewFile/58703/58390.

Still, William. *The Underground Railroad*. Philadelphia: Pennsylvania Anti-Slavery Society, 1872.

Sussex County Court Records. Delaware Public Archives, Dover, Delaware.

Swank, James. *The History of the Manufacture of Iron in All Ages*. Philadelphia: American Iron and Steel Association, 1892.

Torrey, Jesse. *A Portraiture of Domestic Slavery in the United States*. Philadelphia: self-published, John Bioren, Printer, 1817.

Townsend, George Alfred. *Campaigns of a Non-Combatant*. New York: Blelock and Company, 1866.

———. *The Entailed Hat; or, Patty Cannon's Times, A Romance*. New York: Harper and Brothers, Franklin Square, 1884.

———. *Poetical Addresses of Geo. Alfred Townsend*. New York: E.F. Bonaventure and Co., 1881.

Tunnell, James M., Jr. "The Manufacture of Iron in Sussex County." *Delaware History* 4, no. 2 (September 1954).

Turner, C.H.B. *Rodney's Diary and Other Delaware Records*. Philadelphia: Allen, Lane and Scott, 1911.

Turner, Nat. *The Confessions of Nat Turner, The Leader of the Late Insurrection in Southampton, Va*. Richmond: Thomas R. Gray, 1832.

Webster, A.F. "The Delaware Penalties." *Appleton's Journal*, June 20, 1874.

Weems, M.L. "The Life of George Washington." *The Panoplist, and Missionary Magazine United*. Vol. 2. Boston: Farrand, Mallory, and Co., 1810.

Weslager, C.A. *Delaware's Forgotten Folk: The Story of the Moors & Nanticokes*. Philadelphia: University of Pennsylvania Press, 1943.

Williams, William H. *Slavery and Freedom in Delaware, 1639–1865*. Wilmington, DE: Scholarly Resources Inc., 1996.

Wilson, Carol. *Freedom at Risk: The Kidnapping of Free Blacks in America, 1780–1865*. Lexington: University Press of Kentucky, 1994.

Winch, Julie. *A Gentleman of Color: The Life of James Forton*. New York: Oxford University Press, 2002.

———. "Philadelphia and the Other Underground Railroad." *Pennsylvania Magazine of History and Biography* 111, no. 1 (1987).

About the Author

Michael Morgan has been writing freelance newspaper articles on the history of coastal Delaware for over three decades. He is the author of the "Delaware Diary," which appears weekly in the *Delaware Coast Press* and the "Sussex Journal," which is a weekly feature of the *Wave*. Morgan has also published articles in the

The author at Cannon's (Woodland) Ferry. *Photo by Madelyn Morgan.*

America's Civil War, the *Baltimore Sun*, *Chesapeake Bay Magazine*, *Civil War Times*, *Maryland Magazine*, *World War II Magazine* and other national publications. His "Lore of Delmarva" weekly radio commentary on historical topics relating to Maryland and Delaware is broadcast by station WGMD 92.7. Morgan's look at history is marked by a lively, storytelling style that has made his writing and lectures popular. Michael Morgan is also the author of *Pirates and Patriots, Tales of the Delaware Coast*; *Rehoboth Beach, A History of Surf and Sand*; *Bethany Beach, A Brief History*; *Ocean City, Going Down the Ocean*; *Civil War Delaware*; and *Hidden History of Lewes*.

CPSIA information can be obtained
at www.ICGtesting.com
Printed in the USA
BVHW042102060819
555096BV00019BA/1368/P